HIGH EXPECTATIONS
&
FALSE DREAMS

ONE HUNDRED YEARS OF
STOCK MARKET HISTORY
APPLIED TO
RETIREMENT PLANNING

Jim C. Otar
B. A. Sc., M. Eng., CFP

HIGH EXPECTATIONS & FALSE DREAMS

Published in 2001 by
Otar & Associates
96 Willowbrook Road
Thornhill, Canada, L3T 5P5
e-mail: cotar@home.com
www.cotar.org

First Printing: October 2001
Printed in Toronto, Canada by WEBCOM LIMITED

ISBN: 0-9689634-0-4

To my parents, with whom I wish I had spent more time,

and,

To Rita, who has always been beside me.

Author's Preface

This book is based on my research of retirement planning using historic financial data from 1900 to 1999.

As financial advisors, our goal is to provide our clients with realistic retirement projections. My research shows that current models with straight-line growth do not achieve this goal. Adding some randomness to the model, such as the Monte Carlo simulation, is a step in the right direction however, it is still far short of what historic evidence suggests.

This book summarizes the outcome of my research based on empirical data applied to some of the popular portfolio strategies. It shows which techniques work better than others, when and why. There are several worked examples which can guide you when preparing your own retirement plan. Feel free to download my spreadsheet from my website: www.cotar.org.

I had great pleasure writing this book. I hope you'll enjoy reading it.

Jim C. Otar
Toronto, October 1, 2001

Table of Contents

Acknowledgements

I thank my parents Mr. I. Otar and Mrs. H. Otar for their encouragement to write this book. The values and the sense of humour they instilled in the early years of my childhood have been my greatest resources.

Rita, my "better half", asked me a question over a year ago: "Do we have enough to retire on?" As you might expect from an engineer, it took me all this time to review the industry's existing body of knowledge, and not being satisfied with it, spent endless nights to develop the empirical models to search for an answer. I am finally able to answer Rita's question. Only those who know her can appreciate what a relief it is not to let any of her questions go unanswered. I am thankful for her patience and support.

As with my previous book "Commission Free Investing", this book became easier to read because of the valuable suggestions of my friend Diana Wedge. I am fortunate enough to thank her yet again.

I was honoured to find out that the CFP-Board in Denver, U.S.A., unanimously selected my articles on this topic to be among the winners of their 2001 Article Awards Competition. I thank them for their generousity which gave me fresh impetus to complete this book.

Last but not least, I·thank Dale & Betty Ennis for their ongoing friendship. Several years ago, they gave me an opportunity to share my thoughts and findings in their "Canadian MoneySaver" magazine. They always declare: "We pay our writers nothing!" I wish everyone's "nothing" was as generous as Dale & Betty's.

Chapter 1

Introduction

"Wow, it is better than I thought! We won't be broke during our retirement years. Let's hope the markets go up"

It is another one of those nights. Here I am, sitting across the kitchen table with my soon-to-be clients, Dave and Susan[1]. We had our first meeting two weeks ago. During that meeting, I went through a list of standard questions. Dave and Susan spilled out their most confidential information to me. They did it with the hope that, whatever they didn't do for themselves over the years past, the stock market would do for them in the years-to-come.

The chart, their retirement plan, looks impressive. It is even printed in color. It looks as though their retirement assets will be sufficient throughout their retirement. With a little bit of luck, their children may end-up with a small estate. I used a growth rate of 8% for their investments. This is conservative. I have seen many advisors using higher growth rates. Several years ago, while I was still practising engineering, my then-financial advisor used 12% growth in his projections. It did not take me too long to figure out that this number was not realistic.

Dave and Susan are overwhelmed by their retirement plan. They sign the account opening forms with raised hopes mixed with some disbelief. Dave and Susan are now starting on a new journey of high expectations that may last as long as this bull market (this was in 1999). When the next bear market comes around, the chances are, they will look for another financial advisor. They may even decide to look after their finances themselves.

This scenario repeats itself over and over across the kitchen tables or in financial institutions all over the country. It is absurd to believe that after saving for ten or fifteen years, you can expect to live on these investments for twenty-five or thirty years. I sometimes wonder if people will ever realize that there is no such a thing as a 'free lunch'. If I were able to relate this bizarre expectation to my late grandparents, they

---

[1] Names of all persons throughout this book are fictitious.

would laugh themselves to death. They suffered much during the depression years following the 1929 crash.

An investor has three forces working against him:

- The first one is that markets never move on a straight line.
- The second force is one's own greed.
- The third force is the social behaviour of the masses.

The NASDAQ stocks had a stellar rise between September 1999 and March 2000. During a portfolio review meeting in February 2000 with a client, I suggested taking part of the profits and buying some government bonds. In response, he implied that I was trying to sabotage his portfolio. Instead, he signed the waiver instructing me to sell most of his bond holdings and buy more aggressive equity funds. He initiated three errors:

- He ignored the first force that works against him: he thought markets keep "moving up on a straight line".
- He got greedy. He convinced himself that he was "missing the boat".
- He also proved the third force, because "everyone else was doing it".

Any one of these errors has one predictable outcome: the investor loses. Eventually the markets will recover. I am not sure if my client will be there when it happens. He was supposed to retire within a year. After the crash, he decided to work a few more years.

Another story: I interviewed a suspect (i.e. a potential new client) in 1996. He had $20,000 in his open account and about $10,000 in his retirement account with another broker. Three years earlier, he had opened these accounts with about $180,000. He lost apparently more than 80% of his capital since opening these accounts with this broker. This person needed help, so I took over his retirement account. We placed this money into a few diversified mutual funds. The account did reasonably well. Four years later, at the turn of the century, he called me up saying everyone else was buying Nortel, so he wanted to invest all this money in it. First I spoke to him of the virtues of diversification. When this didn't work, I told him that he should take his account elsewhere. He did. Less than a year later, I found out that he lost more than 80% of his investment yet again. In seven years, he experienced losses similar to what occurred during the great depression, *twice*. No one can recover from that.

"If everyone is buying it, then I must be missing something!" The combination of greed and following the like-minded crowd is the most damaging factor to the management of your portfolio. This is so because you can easily justify your errors by simply saying: "Everyone else was doing it!" Investing is not an activity for "me-too's" unless you have relentless discipline and a good understanding of market psychology.

This brings us to retirement plans. Financial advisors of all stripes across the country, produce retirement plans for their clients. These plans can certainly give a useful perspective for retirement planning. In reality, many use these "plans" as a way of selling dreams. All you have to do is to tweak the projected portfolio growth and the projected inflation by one percent, and "voila", you have an achievable plan. "Save this much a year, take more risk", they say, "and if your portfolio grows by 12% a year, then you'll have enough money to retire at 65 and live happily ever after."

To protect the preparer, all respectable retirement plans include a disclaimer, something like "markets are subject to fluctuation and future performance may differ from historic data". The wording of some of the disclaimers might even give an unsuspecting client the impression that, the past performance was so good that the future performance may fail to measure up to it.

Some financial plans go further than that: they show you the historic fluctuations of your selected asset mix during the last twenty or thirty years but they fail to incorporate the adverse effects of such volatility into your plan. An investor is led to believe that if only he/she follow a "buy-and-hold" strategy, things would smooth out over the long term. While this may be correct if you do not need any income from your portfolio, if you do need to draw a regular income from your investments it will deplete your portfolio a lot sooner than you think.

Few financial plans mention a "Monte Carlo" model. This model incorporates random fluctuations to investment return. The fundamental weakness of the Monte Carlo model is that it assumes that all market behaviour is random. There is abundant research[2] that shows that the markets are random only up to a certain point. After that point, they are not random. At these times, good news begets good news (occasionally everyone is rushing to buy because the price is going up) and conversely that bad news begets more bad news (occasionally everyone is rushing to sell because the price is going down). These events frequently occur at the end of bull or bear markets, respectively.

Picture this: You are watching different animals grazing in the African plains from the safety and comfort of your safari vehicle. Hundreds of zebras, giraffes, gazelles, wildebeest and antelope are grazing. They move about in a *random* fashion, feeding on grass, enjoying their day and playing around. All of a sudden, you hear the roar of a lion at a distance. All animals stop grazing, first they lift their heads fearfully, assess the direction of the lion's roar, then they start running away from where the lion's roar originated. Some of the animals that somehow missed the lion's roar at first, now notice that all others are running and they also join this stampede. Once they start running in one direction, theirs is *no longer random* movement. As a matter of fact, if any prey animal is still in its random grazing mode, it will be the dinner for the lion.

Is this scenario similar to market behaviour? You bet. Normally, markets move at random (prey animals grazing). At some point the imbalances build up (the lion gets hungry), stability is disturbed (lion roars). Once the stability is disturbed, then all the movements after that point are non-random (prey animals all running away from the roar of the lion) until the disturbance is exhausted (lion catches one prey animal) and the balance is restored (the lion had her meal). Only after that point, can randomness return (the remaining prey animals start grazing again). This cycle is perpetually repeated. When we talk about a cycle, then we have no choice but to admit the existence of non-randomness.

Luckily for the markets, the periods of non-randomness occur less often than our analogy of the hungry lion. A sustained deviation from randomness can cause a lot of damage to portfolios that are designed based only on the randomness of the markets. Your portfolio, or a good portion of it, may fall prey to non-random events. I don't believe that I

---

[2] An excellent book to read on this subject is "Fractal Market Analysis" by Edgar E. Peters

can, nor should, base my retirement on a random model –like the Monte Carlo model, that has this inherent weakness.

No retirement plan that I have seen depicts a projection of investment assets based on the real history of the capital markets. This is especially important because after retirement, you will likely have little recourse and less opportunity to repair losses to your investment portfolio.

This book is not about how to accumulate assets. That is your problem. There are plenty of books in the marketplace that show you how you can accumulate wealth on a shoestring, or how to pick the next Intel. All this book addresses is that no matter how you accumulated your assets, now you want to preserve them as long as you can.

Neither will I go into the benefits of living frugally or the harm of frivolous spending. You can live frugally and have money until you die, or you can spend frivolously and go broke ten years after your retirement. That is also your choice.

Here, my only goal is to show you how to preserve your capital for as long as you need, based on one hundred years of market behaviour. I wrote this book to help you to see what really would have happened if you retired at anytime during the last century and needed to draw an income from your investment portfolio. It will show you how your investment assets would have held during all the ups and downs, war and peace, bulls and bear markets, inflation and deflation.

The Concept of Portfolio Demand and Supply:

Your investment portfolio has two aspects: Demand and Supply.

Portfolio Demand:

Demand is what you want from your portfolio during your retirement. You may make a statement something like this:

"I have $1,000,000 saved for my retirement. I want to draw $100,000 per year for the next twenty years, adjusted for inflation. I also predict that my equities will outperform the index by 2% each year".

This statement expresses the demand side of your portfolio.

Portfolio Supply:

The supply side is what your portfolio can give you during your retirement based on historic data. This book will tell you:

"You have $1,000,000 for your retirement. You want to draw $100,000 per year adjusted for inflation. During the last century, your optimum asset allocation would have been 60% fixed income and 40% equity. This portfolio would have lasted a minimum of 8½ years. On the average it would have lasted 13 years. After twenty years, the probability of your portfolio being broke would be 95%, even if you had rebalanced it each year."

In recent years, the public has been brainwashed into plunking their money into the stock market and leaving it there. The special interest groups, mainly the media-financial complex, lead the public to have high expectations from the return on equity investments. This book will show you what your portfolio can do for you, based on historic data of the entire twentieth century. It will give you the supply side. It will help you to be realistic about what you can demand from your portfolio. It is entirely based on what we engineers call, empirical data.

This book can help you only if you are willing to learn lessons from history. Since no crystal ball can tell us of the future, for the time being history is our only guide.

Good luck!

Chapter 2

The Last Century

For the average person, the typical life cycle of assets falls into one of the two broad categories: Accumulation and Withdrawal.

Accumulation:

The accumulation phase is when you set aside part of your cash flow for investments. Typical sources for your cash flow are salaries, commissions, bonuses, rental income, royalties, inheritance, business and many income sources during your earning years.

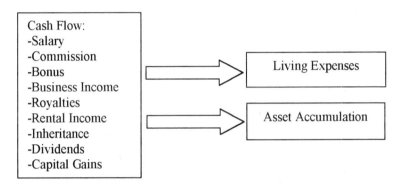

Withdrawal:

The withdrawal phase usually comes after your retirement when (and if) you need income from your assets. You may be using government and private pensions, dividends, rental income and other sources.

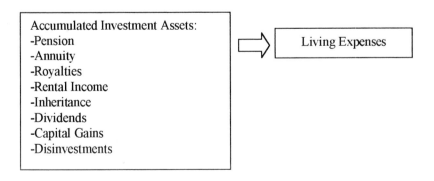

16

All this information is included in the financial[3] plan. The financial plan contains an analysis of cash flow and assets over time. It may also include tax planning and estate planning issues, as well as risk planning (insurance) issues. Here, we are only interested in the relationship between the cash flow and assets in an income portfolio.

The portfolio value over time is typically shown in a single chart called "Investment Assets" (Figure 1)

Investment Assets

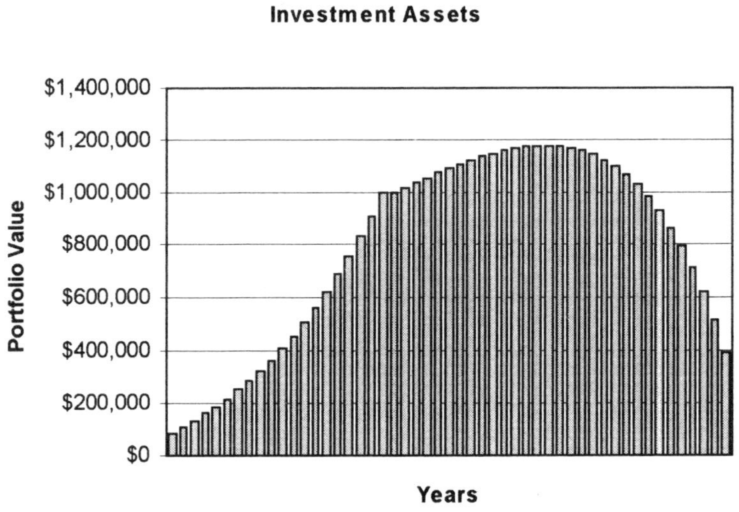

Figure 1: A chart showing the value of investment assets over time in a typical financial plan

Typically one accumulates wealth during his/her working years, as shown on the left hand side of the chart. It shows the effect of adding to your investments each year. The growth follows a parabolic path, in theory anyways.

After retirement, one starts withdrawing from this portfolio. In this case, the assets follow a path[4] that initially rises and then gradually falls.

---

[3] Throughout the text, I used the terms "financial plan" and "retirement plan" interchangeably. Generally a financial plan covers the financial aspects of the entire life cycle of a person. The term "retirement plan" covers the time period after one's retirement.

[4] If withdrawals were small, say less than 3%, the curve during the drawdown years would also follow a rising parabolic path.

My study covers only the retirement years. That being the case, we will look at only the right hand side of the chart, the withdrawal phase. Figure 2 depicts the portfolio value over this time period.

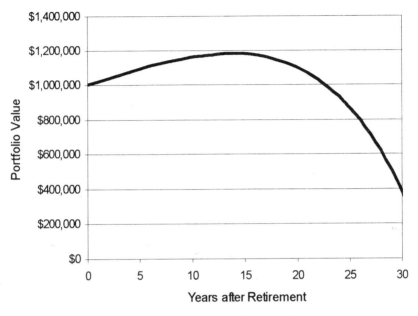

Figure 2:   Portfolio value based on standard retirement plan assumptions

This standard financial plan assumes that you have one million dollars of investment assets at the start of your retirement. Your portfolio will return 8% per year. You want $60,000 from your portfolio in the first year. That means your "initial withdrawal rate" is 6% ($60,000 is 6% of one million dollars). Each year you will adjust the withdrawal amount for inflation. Most people use 3.5% as the annual inflation rate which approximates the historic average. These are realistic assumptions.

Based on these assumptions, the standard retirement plan shows a nice smooth line that rises gradually until about fifteen years after your retirement. As years go by, the withdrawals increase because of the inflation. At about the twenty-third year, the portfolio value is projected to drop below one million dollars. Thirty years after your retirement, it still shows about $390,000. This is just fine, because your life expectancy after retirement is about thirty years. Looking at this chart, with a sigh of relief you conclude that your million-dollar portfolio should last you over your lifetime.

Here is how this standard financial plan projects the portfolio value over time as shown in Figure 2:

Year	Begin Value $	Growth $	Withdrawal $	End Value $
1	1,000,000	80,000	60,000	1,020,000
2	1,020,000	81,600	62,100	1,039,500
3	1,039,500	83,160	64,274	1,058,387
4	1,058,387	84,671	66,523	1,076,534
5	1,076,534	86,123	68,851	1,093,806
6	1,093,806	87,504	71,261	1,110,049
7	1,110,049	88,804	73,755	1,125,098
8	1,125,098	90,008	76,337	1,138,769
9	1,138,769	91,101	79,009	1,150,862
10	1,150,862	92,069	81,774	1,161,157
11	1,161,157	92,893	84,636	1,169,413
12	1,169,413	93,553	87,598	1,175,368
13	1,175,368	94,029	90,664	1,178,734
14	1,178,734	94,299	93,837	1,179,195
15	1,179,195	94,336	97,122	1,176,409
16	1,176,409	94,113	100,521	1,170,001
17	1,170,001	93,600	104,039	1,159,561
18	1,159,561*	92,765	107,681	1,144,646
19	1,144,646	91,572	111,449	1,124,768
20	1,124,768	89,981	115,350	1,099,399
21	1,099,399	87,952	119,387	1,067,964
22	1,067,964	85,437	123,566	1,029,835
23	1,029,835	82,387	127,891	984,331
24	984,331	78,747	132,367	930,711
25	930,711	74,457	137,000	868,168
26	868,168	69,453	141,795	795,827
27	795,827	63,666	146,758	712,736
28	712,736	57,019	151,894	617,860
29	617,860	49,429	157,210	510,079
30	510,079	40,806	162,713	388,173

As comforting as this plan appears, let's compare this with reality. Let's apply the real market data and real inflation and see what happens.

Market History: I used the historic data of Dow Jones Industrial Average[5] (DJIA) to measure the growth of the equity portfolio. It is the only readily available measure of stock market performance covering the entire one hundred years. I could have used the broader S&P 500 index, but then this index did not start until 1926. Using 1926 as my starting year would cover only three years between 1926 and 1929 that ended in the black hole called the "Great Depression". That would unfairly exclude too many of the years prior to the "Great Depression". Excluding them would be a convenient way of avoiding many of the bad years and the outcome of such an analysis would be too optimistic.

Inflation: All withdrawals are adjusted for historic inflation, not an average number. I used the annual average wholesale price index by the U.S. Bureau of Labour Statistics for the years between 1900 and 1913. For the years after 1913, I used the consumer price index from the same source.

Interest Rate: The nominal interest rates are the total return from investing for six months at the beginning of January and July each year from "Market Volatility" by Robert Shiller[6].

In retirement portfolios, the fixed income portion of the portfolio mostly consist of some combination of money market funds, bond ladder, treasury bills etc. Since bonds are usually held until maturity in an income portfolio, I added one percent to the historic 6-month interest rate to estimate the approximate return of the whole fixed income portion of the portfolio.

Diversification: For diversification over different asset classes, I invested 40% of these assets in equities and 60% in fixed income. This asset mix is rebalanced each year. Rebalancing means if equities are more than 40% of my portfolio at the end of the year, then I sell some to bring it back to 40%. The proceeds of this sale are then invested in fixed income. If equities are less than 40% of my portfolio at the end of the year, then I sell some of the fixed income and invest that money in equities bringing

---

[5]   Dow Jones Industrial Average is developed, maintained and licensed by Dow Jones Indexes, part of Dow Jones & Company, Inc.

[6]   The data is courtesy of "Market Volatility" by Robert J. Shiller, MIT Press [1997], page 440-441, Data Series 4. In his book Shiller used data from the Federal Reserve Bulletin starting 1938. For data before 1938, he used Frederick MacCauley's "Some Theoritical Problems Suggested by the Movements of Interest Rates, Bond Yields and Stock Prices since 1856" [1938], Table 10, pp A142-A160.

them back to 40%. In other words, at the end of each year I bring the asset mix ratio back to 40% in equities and 60% in fixed income. It is assumed that the fixed income portion of the portfolio is divided between bonds and short term investments.

Here is what actually happened (Figure 3) if you retired at the beginning of each of the years 1900, 1901, 1902, 1903, etc. during the twentieth century:

Figure 3:   Portfolio value (40% equity, 60% fixed income, rebalanced annually) based on actual historic data during the twentieth century. The heavy line represents the standard retirement plan projection.

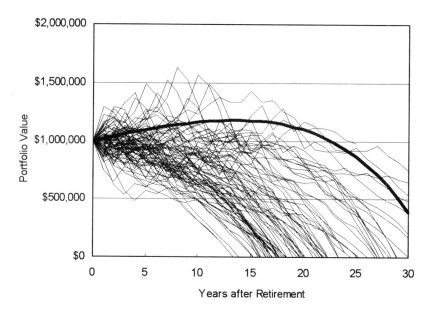

Each line represents the portfolio value of someone who retired in each of the years between 1900 and 1979. Each one shows at least 20 years of history. In other words, if I retired in 1979, the portfolio value between 1979 and 1999 is shown. If I retired in 1933, the portfolio value between 1933 and 1963 is shown. And, so on. For comparison, I included the standard retirement plan with a heavier line in the same chart. After thirty years in only four times out of seventy did the real life portfolio beat the standard retirement plan projection. In sixty-six cases out of seventy, the standard financial plan was far too optimistic.

The initial withdrawal rate in all portfolios was 6%. Initial withdrawal rate is defined as the withdrawal rate in the first year as a percentage of the total investment portfolio. After the first year, the withdrawals are adjusted for annual inflation. So if you have one million dollars to start with, at a 6% initial withdrawal rate you would withdraw $60,000 from your portfolio in the first year. In the following years, the dollar amount of your withdrawals is adjusted to account for inflation. The value of your portfolio will also vary according to market conditions. Nevertheless, the initial withdrawal rate remains at 6%.

Later on, I will talk about the "current withdrawal rate". It is the withdrawal amount in the current year divided by the portfolio value in the current year. The current withdrawal rate is identical to the initial withdrawal rate only in the first year of your retirement.

While we are at it let's look at some more cases. Let's say that because the real-life balanced portfolio was disappointing, I take a bigger risk and invest everything in equities. Figure 4 shows the portfolio value based on historic data. After thirty years in only seven times out of seventy, the real life portfolio beat the standard retirement plan projection. In sixty-three cases out of seventy the standard financial plan was too optimistic. That does not look good either, does it?

Figure 4: Portfolio value of an all equity portfolio based on actual historic data

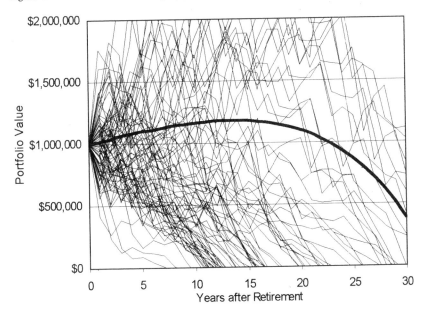

Let's try the opposite. Assume now that I go for safety and only want fixed income in my portfolio. I am holding a mixture of money market funds and mid-term bonds held till maturity. Figure 5 shows the portfolio value based on historic data. After thirty years in only twice out of seventy times does the real life portfolio beat the standard retirement plan projection.

Figure 5:   Portfolio value of an all fixed income portfolio based on actual historic data

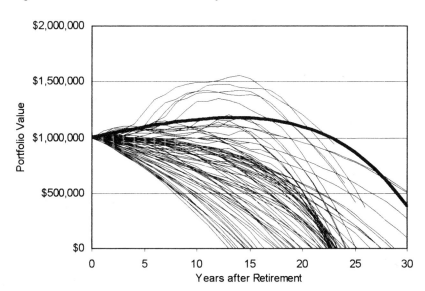

Entertaining isn't it? Not if *you* were the retiree who relied on your standard retirement plan projection.

Let's go back to our balanced portfolio of 40% equity and 60% fixed income. Let's say that in addition to performing exactly the same as DJIA, my equities yield a dividend of 1.5%. This number happens to be the average dividend yield after 1990. Figure 6 shows the portfolio value based on historic data.

Compared to our original balanced portfolio with no dividends (as depicted in Figure 3) there is some improvement. In this case in eight times out of seventy did the portfolio outperform the standard retirement plan. Some improvement, but it is still far from my comfort zone.

Figure 6: Portfolio value of a balanced portfolio (40% equity, 60% fixed income, rebalanced annually) based on actual historic data and equities yield 1.5% dividend

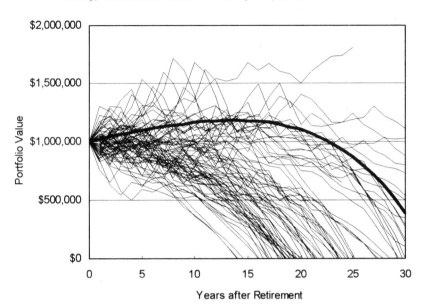

What about equity mutual funds? Over the long term, the actively managed "average" equity mutual funds underperform the benchmark by about 2% per year. Figure 7 shows the portfolio value based on holding "average" equity mutual funds in your portfolio.

As you can see in Figure 7, if you were holding "average" equity funds, *never* in any thirty-year time period did your portfolio outperform the standard retirement plan. In *all* cases, your standard retirement plan was too optimistic.

Is that scary enough?

Figure 7: Portfolio value of a balanced portfolio (40% equity, 60% fixed income, rebalanced annually) based on actual historic data and equities in the portfolio underperforming the DJIA by 2%

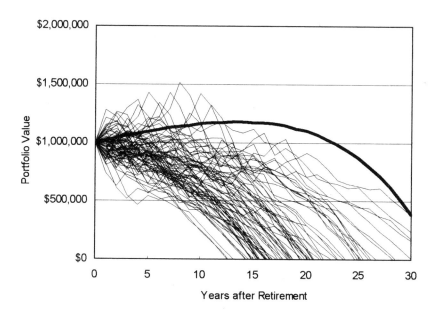

When we focus on the reality and go back to our basic portfolio depicted in Figure 3, we see some frightening scenes. Let's review each of these points:

Volatility:

Most disclaimers in a standard financial plan say something like "the market value of investments may fluctuate". That is an understatement.

- Only four years into retirement, there was already one case where the portfolio value decreased by over 50%. That means your current withdrawal rate effectively jumped from 6% to over 12%. We will later see that when the current withdrawal rate is 12%, the portfolio will deplete on average in eight years.

- We had one case where the portfolio value increased by 40%. That means there was a 90% spread between the high and the low portfolio value in just four years!

Portfolio Life:

Here is another shocker.

- Your standard financial plan showed that you'd have some money left for your estate after thirty years. In reality, you may have nothing left in as little as thirteen years.

- The bulk of the portfolios ran out of money in twenty years. The other times that the portfolio depleted were near the 22nd and 27th years.

- In only seven times out of seventy was there anything left in the portfolio after thirty years.

Standard Financial Plan:

Does it look too optimistic to you too?

- At the end of twenty years, there were only two cases (1919 and 1975, to be exact) out of a possible eighty, when the real life portfolio outperformed the standard financial plan model.

- At the end of twenty-five years, there were only three cases (1919, 1921 and 1975) out of a possible seventy-five when the real life portfolio outperformed the standard financial plan model.

- At the end of thirty years, there were only four cases (1918, 1919, 1920 and 1921) out of a possible seventy years when the real life portfolio outperformed the standard financial plan model.

Why is it that the standard financial plan is so far from the reality? Are financial models designed to mislead investors? Probably not. It is just that the last mega bull market blindsided most people, investors and financial professionals alike. In such euphoria it is easy to extrapolate optimism and overlook reality.

There are several reasons for existing financial plan models to miss reality. They are: Market Cycles, Random Fluctuations, Dollar-Cost Averaging, and Inflation.

Let's look at each of one of these points.

Market Cycles:

Standard financial plans assume a steady growth rate of the equity markets. There is a problem with this assumption: Equity values do not grow steadily, they fluctuate. I don't mean the daily, weekly or monthly random fluctuations (which can also wreak havoc in your portfolio occasionally). I mean the business cycles. Since 1854, the average business cycle lasted 53 months, the average bull market was 35 months and the average bear market was 18 months in duration[7].

Between 1945 and 1991, the average bull market was 50 months, and the average bear market was 11 months. Figure 8 shows the difference between:

- Steady growth rate, as assumed in most standard retirement plans,
- Steady growth rate superimposed with Monte Carlo random fluctuation, as modelled in some retirement plans,
- Typical growth rate with average market cycles, and
- Typical growth rate with average market cycles superimposed with random fluctuations

The market cycles must be incorporated into your retirement plan. It makes a big difference whether you start your retirement at the start of a bear market or a bull market. Withdrawals during a bear market can deplete your portfolio much sooner than you would have imagined prior to reading this book.

I constructed a retirement model that incorporates typical market cycles with random volatility. This model reflects the reality somewhat better than existing models. Figure 9 shows the effects of retiring at the start of a typical bull market and at the start of a typical bear market. In this case, I used an initial withdrawal rate of 6.5%, the annual portfolio growth of 8% and the annual inflation rate of 3.5%.

You may want to visit my site www.cotar.org and download my retirement simulator. Be aware that it does not address the mega bull/bear markets, only the historic minimum portfolio life. Use it at your own risk.

[7] National Bureau of Economic Research, "U.S. Business Cycle Expansions and Contractions", www.nber.org/cycles.html

27

Figure 8: Growth rate models (portfolio value on a logarithmic scale)

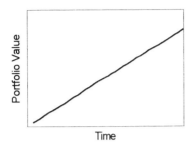

Standard financial plan model
with steady growth

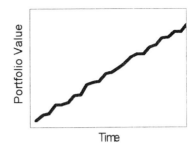

Standard financial plan model
with steady growth and random
volatility (Monte Carlo model)

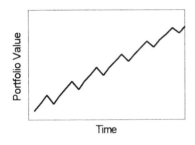

Market cycle model

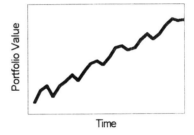

Market cycle model with random
volatility. The randomness is superimposed on the market cycle

28

Figure 9. Retirement projections based on market cycles

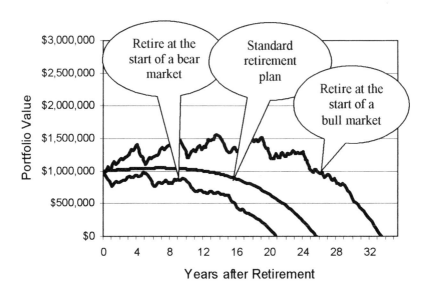

Here, we observe:

- The "standard" retirement plan projected that your assets will last about twenty-six years.

- If you were to retire just before the start of a bull market cycle, the market-cycle model projected that your assets would deplete after about thirty-three years.

- If you retired just before the start of a bear market, you would likely run out of money after about twenty years. As it works out, if you wanted your assets to last as long as your "standard" retirement plan had projected, you would need either 18% more capital ($1,180,000) to start with, or you could take a pay cut of about 14% ($9,000) for the rest of your life, or you could delay your retirement by about three to four years. The other alternative would be to die six years sooner.

While the market-cycle retirement model can produce a more accurate projection than the standard retirement model, it does not handle the "megatrends". If a retiree is caught in a bear megatrend then the projections of this model will still be too optimistic. A bear market megatrend can destroy your income portfolio quickly. What is a megatrend anyway?

Megatrends:

Extended bull or bear markets that are unusual in their severity or longevity are called megatrends. During the last century, we had three bull megatrends with twenty years between each:

- 1920 to 1929   Post World War I era
- 1949 to 1962   Post World War II era
- 1982 to 2000   Post Cold War era

We also had two bear megatrends:

- 1929-1933:   An 80% drop from the end of 1928 to the end of 1932. The depression was technically over in 1933, but the bear market did not really end until World War II.
- 1966-1981:   Essentially no growth of the index for about 16 years.

It appears that during the last century every generation got the chance to experience a bull megatrend. Unfortunately, they also experienced the subsequent bear megatrend.

In bull megatrends, the bear markets are short-lived and shallow. "Buy-and-hold" becomes the general consensus among investors and advisors.

In bear megatrends, the bull markets are short-lived and weak. In such markets, most investors just give up after some trying and move on to other types of endeavors such as real estate, bank deposits, gold or they simply concentrate more on their day jobs.

If we assume an initial withdrawal rate of 6%, an all-equity portfolio would be depleted in about 7 years if one retired at the beginning of 1929, and in about 11 years if one retired at the beginning of 1966.

Even a balanced portfolio (50/50 equity/fixed income) was depleted in about 16.5 years if one retired at the beginning of 1929, and 14.8 years if one retired at the beginning of 1966, 1968 or 1969.

A megatrend exerts one of the biggest influences on the longevity of an income portfolio.

Random Fluctuations:

In addition to cyclical megatrends and market cycles, share prices fluctuate randomly. When I added random fluctuations to my market-cycle model, it showed clearly their effect on the portfolio life. I ran several hundred simulations. At best, the portfolio life increased by 9.4%. At worst it decreased by 7.5%. So random fluctuations, although not the largest contributor to the longevity of your portfolio, make some difference.

Some newer financial plan models include the "Monte Carlo" simulation. The "Monte Carlo" model picks up *only* this type of randomness and this may give you a false sense of security. The main flaw of the Monte Carlo Simulation is that it does not account for cyclical events.

Dollar-Cost Averaging:

Dollar-Cost Averaging (DCA) is defined as adding to, or withdrawing from your investments, a set dollar amount on a periodic basis. One of the main causes of portfolio depletion is the periodic withdrawals during a bear market. The best way of explaining this is through an example.

Let's say you hold an investment that goes through a bear market cycle. The share price first goes down and then goes back up.

Buying on Dollar-Cost Averaging:

We initially invest $500 and then periodically add $60 to this investment over time. Initially, the share price is $10. During the bear market the share price goes down. From there, it gradually recovers back to $10.

Period	Share Price	Transaction Amount	Total Cost	No. of Shares Traded	Share Balance	Total Market Value
Start	$10	$500	$500	50.00	50.00	$500
1	$7	$60	$560	8.57	58.57	$410
2	$8	$60	$620	7.50	66.07	$529
3	$9	$60	$680	6.67	72.74	$655
Final	$10	$60	$740	6.00	78.74	$787

Profit due to DCA at the end of the period: 6.4%

Since both the starting and final share price are the same, i.e. $10, all of the profit is attributable only to the mathematics of DCA. How much is the profit? Because we bought more shares when the price was low for the same $60 periodic investment, when the price went back up to $10, we had more shares to participate in the rise. At the end of the cycle, we read from the last line that our total cost was $740 and the total market value was $787. Therefore, we can calculate the net profit due to DCA as 6.4%, calculated as ($787 / $740-1) x 100%.

Withdrawing on Dollar-Cost Averaging:

Let's say we start with $500 initially and instead of adding $60, we withdraw $60 at each period. We have essentially the same table as above except for the "Transaction Amount" column. The $60 is now replaced with minus $60 because now we are withdrawing from our investment.

Period	Share Price	Transaction Amount	Total Cost	No. of Shares Traded	Share Balance	Total Market Value
Start	$10	$500	$500	50.00	50.00	$500
1	$7	-$60	~~$560~~ 440	-8.57	41.43	$290
2	$8	-$60	~~$620~~ 380	-7.50	33.93	$271
3	$9	-$60	~~$680~~ 320	-6.67	27.26	$245
Final	$10	-$60	~~$740~~ 260	-6.00	21.26	~~$787~~ 213

Loss due to DCA at the end of the period: 18.1%

How much is the loss? Because we had to sell more shares when the price was low for the same $60 periodic withdrawal, when the price went back up to $10, we had less shares to participate in the rise. At the end of the cycle we read from the last line that our total cost is $260, the total market value is $213 and therefore net loss due to DCA is a whopping 18.1%, calculated as ($213 / $260 –1) x 100%.

Granted, this example may be somewhat extreme, to demonstrate my point. However, you don't have to be a genius to see that you can deplete a good portion of your portfolio because you will, in all likelihood, endure three or four bear markets during your retirement.

Inflation:

Retiring at the beginning of a bear market can cause the most damage to your income portfolio. The good thing about it is that it is visible and perhaps you can adjust your lifestyle or you may have some control over the timing of your retirement.

On the other hand, the inflation is the silent killer of a portfolio. Usually, it creeps up slowly over time. It forces you to withdraw more and more income from your portfolio, especially in the later years of your retirement.

On a year-to-year basis, you may not notice the effect of inflation. However, over time, inflation is a real portfolio buster in two ways: firstly, you withdraw more and more from your investments to meet your increasing living expenses. Secondly, to fight inflation, central banks occasionally increase short-term interest rates. This invariably pushes down the share prices, which in turn reduces the value of your investments at least temporarily. Inflation hits you when you may be most vulnerable.

The average historic rate of inflation is about 3.5% per year. At this rate you need to double your withdrawals after 20 years.

Here is a real-life example: Assume you retired at the beginning of 1968 with one million dollars in your portfolio. Your asset allocation was conservative: 60% fixed income and 40% equity. Say your choice of equities outperformed the Dow Jones Industrial Average by 3% each year. You rebalance your portfolio each year.

So you covered all of the bases: conservative asset allocation and good investment performance.

How many years do you think your portfolio would last?

After eleven years, just to keep up with the cost of living, your withdrawals had to double. Seventeen years after your retirement, they had to triple.

	Year	Annual Withdrawal	Portfolio Value at the end of the year
1	1968	$60,000	$1,012,096
2	1969	$63,720	$953,969
3	1970	$67,288	$974,380
4	1971	$69,509	$979,324
5	1972	$71,872	$1,009,353
6	1973	$78,125	$930,465
7	1974	$87,734	$818,429
8	1975	$93,788	$900,389
9	1976	$98,383	$913,328
10	1977	$104,975	$790,643
11	1978	$114,423	$717,405
12	1979	$129,641	$659,534
13	1980	$145,847	$609,947
14	1981	$158,827	$504,096
15	1982	$164,862	$431,997
16	1983	$171,127	$327,953
17	1984	$177,801	$173,010
18	1985	$184,557	$19,376
19	1986	$171,127	$0

In the tenth year, your current withdrawal rate was 13.3%, calculated as:

$$(\$104,975 \, / \, \$790,643) \times 100\% = 13.3\%$$

Anytime this number is above 12%, it should ring alarm bells.

Even the mega-bull markets, which started in 1982, could not compensate for the increased withdrawals. The fact that your equities outperformed the DJIA by 3% each year could not prevent your portfolio's depletion. The interest rates were at an historic high after 1978 but even that did not help much.

The bottom line is that in spite of doing everything right, your one-million-dollar balanced portfolio was totally depleted after eighteen years. By the way, your standard retirement plan model projected a portfolio value of over $1,100,000 for your 18th year of retirement.

The main culprit, in this case, was inflation. Take away the excess inflation[8], and reduce the high interest rates that go with it, and this portfolio would have chugged along just fine for over twenty-five years. This would have been a remarkable achievement considering that you had retired just at the beginning of a mega bear market.

Do governments like high inflation? No, mostly they don't.

Can it happen? Of course it can.

During the twentieth century, high inflation regimes occurred during World War I, at the end of World War II and after the Middle East Crisis of 1973-74 and lasted until 1982.

---

[8] i.e. using the 3.5% average inflation

Chapter 3
The Probability of Going Broke

In this chapter, we'll look at different portfolio combinations and the probability of depletion of an income portfolio based on historic data of 20th century.

I considered a wide range of initial withdrawal rates[9] and I looked at different mixes of equity and fixed income. I also rebalanced each portfolio annually.

The performance of the equity portion of the portfolio may vary widely. This has a large influence on portfolio longevity. You may be holding mutual funds or you may hold dividend-paying stocks. Either may outperform or underperform the index. I therefore looked at a range of relative performance with respect to the DJIA.

If you are holding stocks:

The average annual dividend yield throughout most of the twentieth century was about 4%. After 1990, the average dividend yield declined rapidly to about 1.5% per year. In the future we can expect one of two scenarios: If the average growth rate of the economy continues to be higher than what it was prior to the 1990's, then the average dividend yield should remain where it is now. On the other hand, if the future growth rate is lower than the 1990's, then we cannot expect the stellar returns of the last mega bull market to resume quickly. In fact, continued reduced expectations may cause a market slump that may last until the next mega bull market, whenever that may come. If we assume that the most recent mega bull market died in the year 2000, then based on the history of cycles, does it mean that we have to wait until 2020 for the next mega bull market?

A prudent investor should not count on an overall dividend yield that is higher than 2% for his/her retirement planning projections[10].

---

[9] Remembering that the "initial withdrawal rate" means the withdrawal rate in the first year as a percentage of the total investment portfolio. After the first year, the withdrawals are adjusted for inflation each year.

[10] The average return of DJIA throughout twentieth century was about 8% per year. A 2% average dividend would then bring the average total return to about 10% per year.

If you are holding mutual funds:

Here is the key question: Are your funds outperforming the market? Statistically, it takes several years of history[11] to adequately demonstrate that the fund manager has talent in beating the markets. Any appearance of talent in a shorter time period may be just luck. We have to measure the "short-term talent and/or luck" in a different manner. Chapter 9 covers how to select mutual funds for your portfolio.

Historically, an actively managed "average" equity mutual fund underperforms its benchmark by about 2%-3%. So the first rule is: Whatever you do, do not own an "average" mutual fund.

Whether you are holding stocks or equity mutual funds, it is important to know if the equity portion of your holdings outperforms the index or not. In my models and throughout this book, I looked at five levels of how the equity portion of your portfolio performs relative to the index:

- Same as the index,
- Outperforms index by 2%
- Outperforms index by 4%, and
- Underperforms index by 2%
- Underperforms index by 4%.

In this case, as in all cases throughout this book, the index is the Dow Jones Industrial Average. If a particular portfolio was never depleted for the study period, then that was noted as "NIL" in the tables below.

In addition to the probability of depletion, each table shows both the minimum and the average number of years that the portfolio would survive. That may give you a better perspective for the worst-case scenarios. When a portfolio life was longer than 40 years, then it was noted as "40+".

In all cases, it is assumed that the retiree holds a bond ladder[12] in the fixed income portion of his/her portfolio. It is also assumed that these bonds are held until maturity. Consequently, I ran all cases with the

---

[11]   This number is somewhere between 14 years and 22 years depending on investment style.

[12]   A bond ladder is a portfolio of bonds with differing maturity dates. For example: a portfolio of three bonds with maturity dates in 2004, 2007, and 2010. As each bond matures, with the proceeds, a new bond with longer maturity is bought. For example: when the first bond matures in 2004, the proceeds are used in a new bond maturing in 2013. Bond ladders smooth out the interest rate risk in the bond portfolio.

assumption that the fixed income portion of the portfolio returned one percent over and above the prevailing 6-month interest rate.

Initial Withdrawal Rate: 3%

ASSET MIX
(%Equity / %Fixed Income)

	100 / 0	60 / 40	40 / 60	20 / 80	0 / 100

Equity Performance: **DJIA + 4%:**

PORTFOLIO LIFE (years)					
Minimum	34.6	40+	40+	37.2	26.9
Average	40+	40+	40+	40+	40+

PROBABILITY OF DEPLETION					
After 5 years	NIL	NIL	NIL	NIL	NIL
After 10 years	NIL	NIL	NIL	NIL	NIL
After 15 years	NIL	NIL	NIL	NIL	NIL
After 20 years	NIL	NIL	NIL	NIL	NIL
After 25 years	NIL	NIL	NIL	NIL	NIL
After 30 years	NIL	NIL	NIL	NIL	11%

Equity Performance: **DJIA + 2%:**

PORTFOLIO LIFE (years)					
Minimum	19.8	40+	40+	33.8	26.9
Average	40+	40+	40+	40+	40+

PROBABILITY OF DEPLETION					
After 5 years	NIL	NIL	NIL	NIL	NIL
After 10 years	NIL	NIL	NIL	NIL	NIL
After 15 years	NIL	NIL	NIL	NIL	NIL
After 20 years	1%	NIL	NIL	NIL	NIL
After 25 years	5%	NIL	NIL	NIL	NIL
After 30 years	10%	NIL	NIL	NIL	11%

Initial Withdrawal Rate: 3%

ASSET MIX
(%Equity / %Fixed Income)

	100 / 0	60 / 40	40 / 60	20 / 80	0 / 100

Equity Performance: **SAME AS DJIA:**

PORTFOLIO LIFE (years)					
Minimum	15.1	30.8	34.3	30.9	26.9
Average	33.2	40+	40+	40+	40+

PROBABILITY OF DEPLETION					
After 5 years	NIL	NIL	NIL	NIL	NIL
After 10 years	NIL	NIL	NIL	NIL	NIL
After 15 years	NIL	NIL	NIL	NIL	NIL
After 20 years	8%	NIL	NIL	NIL	NIL
After 25 years	20%	NIL	NIL	NIL	NIL
After 30 years	36%	NIL	NIL	NIL	11%

Equity Performance: **DJIA - 2%:**

PORTFOLIO LIFE (years)					
Minimum	13.3	24.0	28.8	28.5	26.9
Average	28.7	39.5	40+	40+	40+

PROBABILITY OF DEPLETION					
After 5 years	NIL	NIL	NIL	NIL	NIL
After 10 years	NIL	NIL	NIL	NIL	NIL
After 15 years	2%	NIL	NIL	NIL	NIL
After 20 years	23%	NIL	NIL	NIL	NIL
After 25 years	49%	1%	NIL	NIL	NIL
After 30 years	57%	17%	3%	4%	11%

Equity Performance: **DJIA - 4%:**

PORTFOLIO LIFE (years)					
Minimum	11.8	20.3	24.9	26.6	26.9
Average	22.5	32.5	40.0	40+	40+

PROBABILITY OF DEPLETION					
After 5 years	NIL	NIL	NIL	NIL	NIL
After 10 years	NIL	NIL	NIL	NIL	NIL
After 15 years	13%	NIL	NIL	NIL	NIL
After 20 years	46%	NIL	NIL	NIL	NIL
After 25 years	64%	16%	1%	NIL	NIL
After 30 years	80%	43%	11%	7%	11%

Initial Withdrawal Rate: **4%**

ASSET MIX
(%Equity / %Fixed Income)

	100 / 0	**60 / 40**	**40 / 60**	**20 / 80**	**0 / 100**

Equity Performance: **DJIA + 4%:**

PORTFOLIO LIFE (years)					
Minimum	17.9	38.7	30.4	23.4	19.3
Average	38.1	40+	40+	40+	37.1

PROBABILITY OF DEPLETION					
After 5 years	NIL	NIL	NIL	NIL	NIL
After 10 years	NIL	NIL	NIL	NIL	NIL
After 15 years	NIL	NIL	NIL	NIL	NIL
After 20 years	4%	NIL	NIL	NIL	NIL
After 25 years	8%	NIL	NIL	4%	19%
After 30 years	10%	NIL	NIL	11%	21%

Equity Performance: **DJIA + 2%:**

PORTFOLIO LIFE (years)					
Minimum	14.0	24.1	25.3	22.0	19.3
Average	28.6	40+	40+	40+	37.1

PROBABILITY OF DEPLETION					
After 5 years	NIL	NIL	NIL	NIL	NIL
After 10 years	NIL	NIL	NIL	NIL	NIL
After 15 years	1%	NIL	NIL	NIL	NIL
After 20 years	11%	NIL	NIL	NIL	3%
After 25 years	25%	1%	NIL	7%	19%
After 30 years	36%	10%	6%	14%	21%

Equity Performance: **SAME AS DJIA:**

PORTFOLIO LIFE (years)					
Minimum	12.1	19.8	21.9	20.8	19.3
Average	28.7	34.2	37.2	39.4	37.1

PROBABILITY OF DEPLETION					
After 5 years	NIL	NIL	NIL	NIL	NIL
After 10 years	NIL	NIL	NIL	NIL	NIL
After 15 years	7%	NIL	NIL	NIL	NIL
After 20 years	29%	1%	NIL	NIL	3%
After 25 years	48%	15%	5%	11%	19%
After 30 years	59%	31%	23%	23%	19%

Initial Withdrawal Rate: **4%**

ASSET MIX
(%Equity / %Fixed Income)

	100 / 0	60 / 40	40 / 60	20 / 80	0 / 100

Equity Performance: **DJIA - 2%:**

PORTFOLIO LIFE (years)					
Minimum	10.3	17.5	19.7	19.8	19.3
Average	22.3	29.3	33.4	36.9	37.1

PROBABILITY OF DEPLETION					
After 5 years	NIL	NIL	NIL	NIL	NIL
After 10 years	NIL	NIL	NIL	NIL	NIL
After 15 years	22%	NIL	NIL	NIL	NIL
After 20 years	49%	11%	3%	3%	3%
After 25 years	64%	41%	16%	11%	19%
After 30 years	74%	59%	39%	23%	21%

Equity Performance: **DJIA - 4%:**

PORTFOLIO LIFE (years)					
Minimum	9.0	16.0	17.8	18.9	19.3
Average	18.5	24.2	28.2	33.5	37.1

PROBABILITY OF DEPLETION					
After 5 years	NIL	NIL	NIL	NIL	NIL
After 10 years	1%	NIL	NIL	NIL	NIL
After 15 years	31%	NIL	NIL	NIL	NIL
After 20 years	64%	29%	5%	4%	3%
After 25 years	80%	61%	33%	13%	19%
After 30 years	94%	81%	67%	29%	21%

Example: Say you are holding two portfolios, each with 60% equities and 40% fixed income, and your initial withdrawal rate is 4%.

In the first portfolio, Portfolio "A", your equities consist of equity mutual funds that outperform DJIA by 2%.

In the other portfolio, Portfolio "B", your equities consist of equity mutual funds that underperform DJIA by 2%.

Now, look at the tables with initial withdrawal rate of 4%, after 25 years. Look under the asset mix column of 60/40. Portfolio "A" had a 1% chance of depletion. On the other hand, Portfolio "B" had a 41% chance of depletion.

Which portfolio would you choose?

Initial Withdrawal Rate: **6%**

ASSET MIX
(%Equity / %Fixed Income)

	100 / 0	60 / 40	40 / 60	20 / 80	0 / 100

Equity Performance: **DJIA + 4%:**

PORTFOLIO LIFE (years)					
Minimum	10.3	16.3	15.3	14.0	12.9
Average	21.3	26.7	27.8	25.0	21.7

PROBABILITY OF DEPLETION					
After 5 years	NIL	NIL	NIL	NIL	NIL
After 10 years	NIL	NIL	NIL	NIL	NIL
After 15 years	9%	NIL	NIL	2%	12%
After 20 years	29%	20%	13%	18%	31%
After 25 years	47%	41%	49%	61%	83%
After 30 years	53%	53%	64%	84%	94%

Equity Performance: **DJIA + 2%:**

PORTFOLIO LIFE (years)					
Minimum	8.9	14.5	14.2	13.6	12.9
Average	24.2	26.3	25.1	23.3	21.7

PROBABILITY OF DEPLETION					
After 5 years	NIL	NIL	NIL	NIL	NIL
After 10 years	2%	NIL	NIL	NIL	NIL
After 15 years	25%	5%	4%	4%	12%
After 20 years	50%	36%	33%	24%	31%
After 25 years	59%	59%	65%	72%	83%
After 30 years	63%	70%	76%	89%	94%

Initial Withdrawal Rate: **6%**

ASSET MIX
(%Equity / %Fixed Income)

	100 / 0	60 / 40	40 / 60	20 / 80	0 / 100

Equity Performance: **SAME AS DJIA:**

PORTFOLIO LIFE (years)					
Minimum	7.2	13.2	13.4	13.2	12.9
Average	19.2	21.4	21.9	22.0	21.7

PROBABILITY OF DEPLETION					
After 5 years	NIL	NIL	NIL	NIL	NIL
After 10 years	3%	NIL	NIL	NIL	NIL
After 15 years	36%	18%	4%	6%	12%
After 20 years	59%	53%	46%	40%	31%
After 25 years	73%	73%	73%	76%	83%
After 30 years	84%	83%	89%	90%	94%

Equity Performance: **DJIA - 2%:**

PORTFOLIO LIFE (years)					
Minimum	6.2	12.2	12.6	12.8	12.9
Average	16.1	18.7	19.9	20.9	21.7

PROBABILITY OF DEPLETION					
After 5 years	NIL	NIL	NIL	NIL	NIL
After 10 years	9%	NIL	NIL	NIL	NIL
After 15 years	51%	31%	11%	7%	12%
After 20 years	75%	64%	58%	49%	31%
After 25 years	89%	81%	83%	87%	83%
After 30 years	100%	97%	93%	93%	94%

Equity Performance: **DJIA - 4%:**

PORTFOLIO LIFE (years)					
Minimum	5.4	11.3	11.9	12.5	12.9
Average	13.9	16.8	18.3	20.0	21.7

PROBABILITY OF DEPLETION					
After 5 years	NIL	NIL	NIL	NIL	NIL
After 10 years	24%	NIL	NIL	NIL	NIL
After 15 years	60%	36%	22%	7%	12%
After 20 years	84%	78%	71%	56%	31%
After 25 years	100%	95%	91%	89%	83%
After 30 years	100%	100%	99%	94%	94%

Initial Withdrawal Rate: **8%**

ASSET MIX
(%Equity / %Fixed Income)

	100 / 0	**60 / 40**	**40 / 60**	**20 / 80**	**0 / 100**

Equity Performance: **DJIA + 4%:**

PORTFOLIO LIFE (years)					
Minimum	6.4	11.4	10.9	10.5	10.1
Average	19.7	20.6	18.5	16.9	15.6

PROBABILITY OF DEPLETION					
After 5 years	NIL	NIL	NIL	NIL	NIL
After 10 years	3%	NIL	NIL	NIL	NIL
After 15 years	34%	33%	28%	35%	36%
After 20 years	56%	59%	70%	85%	86%
After 25 years	63%	76%	88%	93%	97%
After 30 years	70%	84%	93%	97%	100%

Equity Performance: **DJIA + 2%:**

PORTFOLIO LIFE (years)					
Minimum	5.6	10.5	10.5	10.3	10.1
Average	17.6	17.4	16.9	16.4	15.6

PROBABILITY OF DEPLETION					
After 5 years	NIL	NIL	NIL	NIL	NIL
After 10 years	14%	NIL	NIL	NIL	NIL
After 15 years	47%	38%	42%	41%	36%
After 20 years	69%	73%	76%	85%	86%
After 25 years	77%	85%	91%	95%	97%
After 30 years	87%	97%	97%	99%	100%

Equity Performance: **SAME AS DJIA:**

PORTFOLIO LIFE (years)					
Minimum	4.7	9.7	10.0	10.1	10.1
Average	14.4	15.4	15.7	15.8	15.6

PROBABILITY OF DEPLETION					
After 5 years	1%	NIL	NIL	NIL	NIL
After 10 years	27%	4%	1%	NIL	NIL
After 15 years	59%	52%	51%	44%	36%
After 20 years	80%	79%	85%	88%	86%
After 25 years	92%	96%	95%	96%	97%
After 30 years	100%	100%	100%	100%	100%

Initial Withdrawal Rate: **8%**

ASSET MIX
(%Equity / %Fixed Income)

	100 / 0	60 / 40	40 / 60	20 / 80	0 / 100

Equity Performance: **DJIA - 2%:**

PORTFOLIO LIFE (years)					
Minimum	4.4	9.1	9.6	9.9	10.1
Average	12.4	14.1	14.6	15.2	15.6

PROBABILITY OF DEPLETION					
After 5 years	2%	NIL	NIL	NIL	NIL
After 10 years	33%	9%	2%	1%	NIL
After 15 years	68%	65%	56%	48%	36%
After 20 years	91%	89%	89%	89%	86%
After 25 years	100%	100%	99%	97%	97%
After 30 years	100%	100%	100%	100%	100%

Equity Performance: **DJIA - 4%:**

PORTFOLIO LIFE (years)					
Minimum	4.1	8.4	9.2	9.7	10.1
Average	11.0	12.9	13.8	14.7	15.6

PROBABILITY OF DEPLETION					
After 5 years	2%	NIL	NIL	NIL	NIL
After 10 years	41%	19%	3%	2%	NIL
After 15 years	82%	71%	67%	58%	36%
After 20 years	100%	98%	93%	89%	86%
After 25 years	100%	100%	100%	99%	97%
After 30 years	100%	100%	100%	100%	100%

Initial Withdrawal Rate: **10%**

ASSET MIX
(%Equity / %Fixed Income)

	100 / 0	**60 / 40**	**40 / 60**	**20 / 80**	**0 / 100**

Equity Performance: **DJIA + 4%:**

PORTFOLIO LIFE (years)					
Minimum	4.5	8.4	8.8	8.6	8.3
Average	16.2	14.7	13.9	13.0	12.4

PROBABILITY OF DEPLETION					
After 5 years	1%	NIL	NIL	NIL	NIL
After 10 years	29%	12%	10%	13%	18%
After 15 years	54%	61%	67%	79%	81%
After 20 years	71%	80%	90%	96%	99%
After 25 years	79%	96%	99%	100%	100%
After 30 years	87%	100%	100%	100%	100%

Equity Performance: **DJIA + 2%:**

PORTFOLIO LIFE (years)					
Minimum	4.3	7.9	8.5	8.4	8.3
Average	13.4	13.2	13.0	12.7	12.4

PROBABILITY OF DEPLETION					
After 5 years	2%	NIL	NIL	NIL	NIL
After 10 years	33%	22%	14%	16%	18%
After 15 years	65%	67%	72%	80%	81%
After 20 years	85%	95%	95%	98%	99%
After 25 years	93%	100%	100%	100%	100%
After 30 years	100%	100%	100%	100%	100%

Equity Performance: **SAME AS DJIA:**

PORTFOLIO LIFE (years)					
Minimum	3.7	7.4	8.2	8.3	8.3
Average	11.5	12.1	12.3	12.5	12.4

PROBABILITY OF DEPLETION					
After 5 years	2%	NIL	NIL	NIL	NIL
After 10 years	41%	32%	22%	19%	18%
After 15 years	78%	74%	79%	81%	81%
After 20 years	94%	99%	98%	98%	99%
After 25 years	100%	100%	100%	100%	100%
After 30 years	100%	100%	100%	100%	100%

Initial Withdrawal Rate: 10%				

ASSET MIX				
(%Equity / %Fixed Income)				
100 / 0	60 / 40	40 / 60	20 / 80	0 / 100

Equity Performance: **DJIA - 2%:**

PORTFOLIO LIFE (years)				
Minimum	3.4	7.0	7.8	8.2	8.3
Average	10.1	11.2	11.8	12.2	12.4

PROBABILITY OF DEPLETION				
After 5 years	2%	NIL	NIL	NIL	NIL
After 10 years	51%	39%	33%	21%	18%
After 15 years	86%	82%	85%	81%	81%
After 20 years	100%	100%	100%	100%	99%
After 25 years	100%	100%	100%	100%	100%
After 30 years	100%	100%	100%	100%	100%

Equity Performance: **DJIA - 4%:**

PORTFOLIO LIFE (years)				
Minimum	3.2	6.6	7.5	8.0	8.3
Average	9.2	10.6	11.2	11.9	12.4

PROBABILITY OF DEPLETION				
After 5 years	3%	NIL	NIL	NIL	NIL
After 10 years	61%	46%	39%	22%	18%
After 15 years	93%	95%	87%	85%	81%
After 20 years	100%	100%	100%	100%	99%
After 25 years	100%	100%	100%	100%	100%
After 30 years	100%	100%	100%	100%	100%

Table 1 (see next page) summarizes the portfolio life for the 60% fixed income and 40% equity mix rebalanced annually. It is the base case for comparing different methods in the following chapters.

Figure 10 (see page 48) compares the portfolio values after retirement for the strategic asset allocation and the 100% equity portfolio. The strategic asset allocation increases the minimum portfolio life when compared with an all-equity portfolio. It also increases the average portfolio life at low withdrawal rates.

Figure 11 (see page 49) compares the portfolio values after retirement for the strategic asset allocation and the 100% fixed income portfolio. The strategic asset allocation increases the minimum portfolio life when compared with an all-fixed income portfolio only at lower withdrawal rates. It does not increase the minimum portfolio life at higher withdrawal rates, neither does it increase the average portfolio life.

For comparison, the heavy solid line in each chart shows the standard retirement plan projection based on an average annual inflation rate of 3.5% and an annual growth rate of 8%.

Table 1: Portfolio Life for Asset Mix of 60% fixed income and 40% equity, rebalanced annually

Equity Performance Relative to DJIA	Initial Withdrawal Rate	Minimum Portfolio Life, years	Average Portfolio Life, years	Probability of Depletion after		
				10 years	20 years	30 years
DJIA + 4%	3%	40+	40+	0%	0%	0%
	4%	30.4	40+	0%	0%	0%
	5%	20.0	35.2	0%	0%	23%
	6%	15.3	27.8	0%	13%	64%
	8%	10.9	18.5	0%	70%	93%
	10%	8.8	13.9	10%	90%	100%
DJIA + 2%	3%	40+	40+	0%	0%	0%
	4%	25.3	40+	0%	0%	6%
	5%	18.1	32.3	0%	4%	46%
	6%	14.2	25.1	0%	33%	76%
	8%	10.5	16.9	0%	76%	97%
	10%	8.5	13.0	14%	95%	100%
DJIA	3%	34.2	40+	0%	0%	0%
	4%	21.9	37.2	0%	0%	23%
	5%	16.4	28.4	0%	9%	69%
	6%	13.4	21.9	0%	46%	89%
	8%	10.0	15.7	1%	85%	100%
	10%	8.2	12.3	22%	98%	100%
DJIA − 2%	3%	28.8	40+	0%	0%	3%
	4%	19.7	33.4	0%	3%	39%
	5%	15.1	24.5	0%	24%	81%
	6%	12.6	19.9	0%	58%	93%
	8%	9.6	14.6	2%	89%	100%
	10%	7.8	11.8	33%	100%	100%
DJIA − 4%	3%	24.9	40.0	0%	0%	11%
	4%	17.8	28.2	0%	5%	67%
	5%	14.2	22.0	0%	41%	90%
	6%	11.9	18.3	0%	71%	99%
	8%	9.2	13.8	3%	93%	100%
	10%	7.5	11.2	39%	100%	100%

48

Figure 10. Portfolio value for retirement years between 1900-1999: Strategic Asset Allocation (60% fixed income, 40% equity, rebalanced annually) versus an all equity portfolio. The heavy line is the standard retirement model.

In all cases, the strategic asset allocation increases the minimum portfolio life when compared with an all-equity portfolio. It also increases the average portfolio life at low withdrawal rates. Even though the all-equity portfolios outperform the strategic asset allocation frequently, in the final analysis the strategic asset allocation outlasts an all-equity portfolio in the long term.

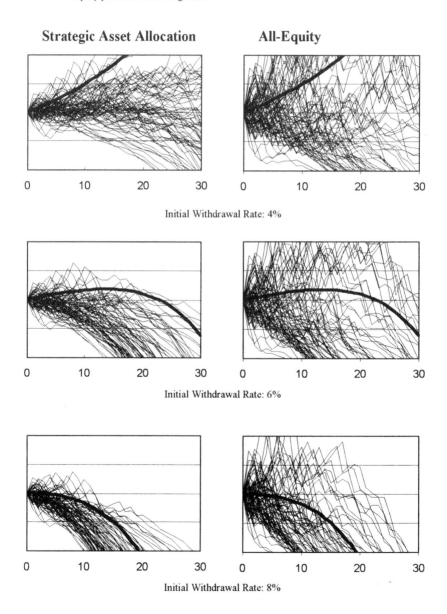

Figure 11. Portfolio value for retirement years between 1900-1999: Strategic Asset Allocation (60% fixed income, 40% equity, rebalanced annually) versus an all fixed income portfolio. The heavy line is the standard retirement model.

The strategic asset allocation increases the minimum portfolio life when compared with an all-fixed income portfolio at lower withdrawal rates. It does not increase the minimum portfolio life at higher withdrawal rates. It does not increase the average portfolio life.

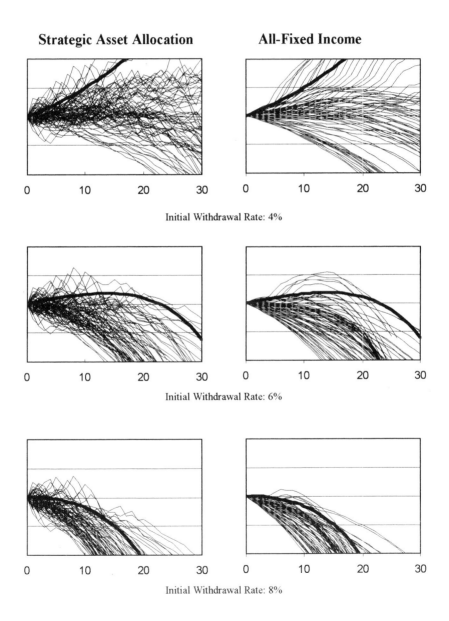

Chapter 4
The Twilight of Your Portfolio

Earlier, I mentioned the definition of "current withdrawal rate", which is the withdrawal amount during the current year divided by the portfolio value. It varies as you change your withdrawals and as your portfolio value changes over time.

As time goes on, you withdraw larger and larger amounts to keep up with the cost of living and therefore, the "current withdrawal rate" usually[13] increases. I observed that whenever the current withdrawal rate exceeded 12%, the portfolio depleted rapidly and decisively. Once this excessive level of withdrawal is reached, the portfolio is on a slippery slope; nothing can prevent it from the eventual collapse except reducing the withdrawals drastically. This eventuality will not change even if a mega bull market subsequently arrived.

The charts in Figure 12 depict the remaining portfolio life as a function of the current withdrawal rate. The horizontal scale shows the current withdrawal rate. Once you determine this withdrawal rate, you can then look-up the range of the remaining portfolio life on the vertical scale. The upper chart shows the observations for an all-equity portfolio and the lower chart, for an all-fixed income portfolio.

The solid line shows the best fitting curve, and the dashed lines show the range of observations.

---

[13]   When the withdrawals are very small (initial withdrawal rate of less than 2%), the current withdrawal rate may decrease over time as the portfolio may grow faster than the withdrawals.

Figure 12: Remaining Portfolio Life at excessive withdrawal rates

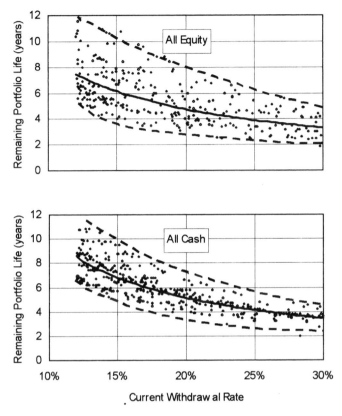

Once you know your current withdrawal rate (CWR) you can then estimate the average, maximum and minimum remaining portfolio life (RPL) of a balanced portfolio with reasonable accuracy using the following equation:

$$RPL, years = \frac{A}{CWR}$$

where:

A is: 100 for average remaining portfolio life
           150 for maximum remaining portfolio life
           75 for minimum remaining portfolio life

CWR is: larger than 12%

For example, if the current withdrawal rate is 15%:

- Average remaining portfolio life is:
  6.7 years, calculated as 100/15
- Maximum remaining portfolio life is:
  10 years, calculated as 150/15
- Minimum remaining portfolio life is:
  5 years, calculated as 75/15

based on one hundred years of history.

A fixed income (marked as " cash" in Figure 12) portfolio has a lower volatility than an equity portfolio. Therefore, the data points for a fixed income portfolio are clustered near the best fitting curve more so than for an equity portfolio. Consequently, at excessive withdrawal rates a fixed income portfolio follows a more predictable remaining portfolio life than an equity portfolio.

Switching to Cash in Final Years:

Since fixed income portfolios produce a more predictable outcome at excessive withdrawal levels, I wanted to study the effect of switching to cash in the final years of a portfolio. My first instinct was that doing so would protect the portfolio from further volatility of the equity market. I was expecting that this would result in a longer portfolio life.

In my models, I built an option to switch everything to cash as soon as the current withdrawal rate exceeded a specified level. I tried 12%, 20%, 25% and 30%. I was surprised to see that in almost all cases, switching everything to cash shortened the portfolio life even more.

One explanation for this might be, that many times the reason that the current withdrawal rate goes above 12% is the result of a sharp drop in the equity markets. If you then switch everything to cash, you may miss the subsequent potential rise in equities.

So the lesson is that even at excessive withdrawal rates, it is better to stick with the original asset mix.

Chapter 5
Optimizing Strategic Asset Allocation

In Chapter 3, we saw the tables showing the probability of depletion as well as the average and minimum portfolio life for various asset mixes, initial withdrawal rates, relative performance and time periods.

In this chapter we'll look at optimizing the asset mix. We will also investigate different rebalancing methods.

Let's first define strategic asset allocation: Strategic asset allocation means establishing a suitable mix of cash, fixed income and equities in a portfolio and maintaining it over time. Equities, bonds and cash behave differently during different market environments and they are called asset classes. By investing in different asset classes, your risk is reduced. Over time, the percentages of this mix will change with market conditions. In a process called rebalancing the holdings are adjusted to bring the current asset mix back to its original percentages. Rebalancing involves selling some of the assets of the asset class that did better and buying more of the asset class that performed less well during the preceding time period.

The first step in strategic asset allocation is to establish your risk tolerance. This is done through a series of questions. Your answers to these questions will place you, the investor, into one of the four or five categories. Depending on the category in which you fit, your "ideal" asset mix of equity, bond and cash is determined. Your money is then invested according to this ideal asset mix. Subsequently, your portfolio is rebalanced periodically, usually annual and sometimes more frequently.

Strategic Asset Allocation is easy to implement and to maintain. This is one of the reasons why it is so popular in the financial planning community as compared to other methods such as market timing.

A typical flaw in this process is that investors are more aggressive during bull markets so when they fill out their risk questionnaire their answers place them into more aggressive portfolio categories. When markets turn sour the investor takes a larger hit. They then become more conservative, rearrange their portfolio, (perhaps change advisors too) and miss the subsequent rise in the markets. And so goes the cycle.

Strategic asset allocation attempts to reduce the volatility of investment returns. It works well during wealth creation; by keeping the portfolio volatility to within the tolerable levels, the investor is encouraged to continue accumulating wealth through the ups and downs of the markets.

The problem starts when the same philosophy is applied to an income portfolio where the primary objective is different. The goal in an income portfolio is not accumulation but preservation. Therefore, one must be very careful to take out the periodic withdrawals *only* from the cash portion of the portfolio.

Optimizing the Asset Allocation:

Going back one hundred years, I ran several "what-if" scenarios. These scenarios produced different portfolio profiles at different initial withdrawal rates and with different asset allocations. Figures 13 and 14 show typical portfolio profiles with 3% and 6% initial withdrawal rates, respectively.

The upper chart shows the probability of portfolio depletion for different asset mixes after 5, 10, 15, 20, 25, 30 years. The bottom chart shows the average and the minimum life of the portfolio for each asset mix.

A visual inspection of the portfolio profile will usually reveal the optimum asset allocation. The first step is to look for the lowest probability of depletion. If we look at the upper chart in Figure 13, we see that the minimum occurs at an asset mix of 60% fixed income and 40% equity. We observe that even the 30-year profile (the line with "o"s on it), has zero percent probability of depletion at this optimum asset mix. If you change the asset mix in either direction then the probability of depletion increases.

We confirm this finding by looking at the lower chart: The minimum portfolio life (the line with little triangles) also peaks at the same asset mix of 60% fixed income and 40% equity. This finding confirms that not only at this asset mix do we have the minimum probability of depletion, but we also have the longest minimum portfolio life.

Figure 13. Portfolio Profile for all years 1900-1999, 3% Initial Withdrawal Rate, 0% bond premium (fixed income is all in cash)

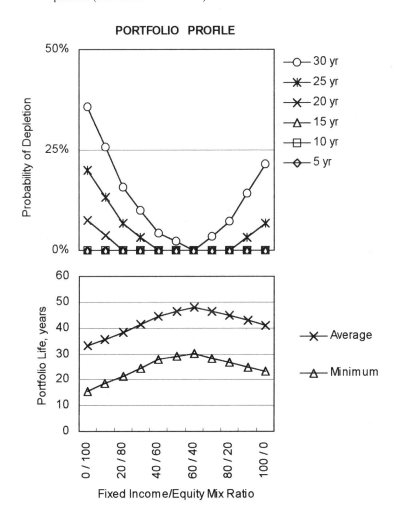

Now we have our optimum asset allocation. It has nothing to do with how old you are, what your investment knowledge is, or how much of a risk-taker you are. Countless questions that you answered when you filled out your risk profile questionnaire are totally irrelevant to your optimum income portfolio. The only purpose of the whole ritual of risk profile assessment is perhaps to fulfill the demands of the regulators[14],

---

[14]   The term regulator is used here to describe the supervisory body of securities markets.

to attempt to prevent some rogue and/or inexperienced advisor ruining your assets and to cover the back of the investment professional.

The fact is that without knowing *anything at all* about you except your withdrawal rate (in this case it was 3%), one could have invested all your money in an asset mix of 60% fixed income and 40% equity in the beginning of 1929 and your portfolio would have generated an income, adjusted for inflation, for 43 years and 8 months. Remarkable!

Figure 14. Portfolio Profile for all years 1900-1999, 6% Initial Withdrawal Rate

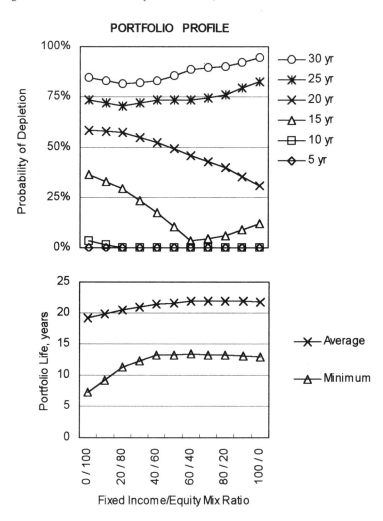

I mentioned the demand and the supply side of an income portfolio earlier, in Chapter 1. The demand side is what *you want* from your portfolio during your retirement. The supply side is what your portfolio *can do for you* during your retirement based on historic data.

When looking at the optimum asset allocation for an income portfolio, the only variable on the demand side is the income, so all we need to know is the withdrawal rate. This alone will give us sufficient information to estimate the supply side, i.e. what the markets can do for you.

The secondary variable is the life expectancy. With the optimum portfolio if the life expectancy of the retiree is longer than what the optimum portfolio can provide, then other avenues of planning such as annuities or reducing the amount of withdrawals should be investigated.

The life of an income portfolio depends on the withdrawal rate. Even if you use the best of techniques and methods, you cannot make an income portfolio survive thirty years if your withdrawals are 10% per year. It just has never happened during the last century. It does not matter how old you are or how long you plan to live. The markets don't know and don't care about you. All they, the markets, say is: "This is what we gave you during the past". You have to arrange your finances so that you can make the best of what the markets can give you.

Too many advisors and investors confuse the demand and the supply side of an income portfolio. They may say to a retiree something to the effect of: "You need to take higher risk (i.e. buy more equities) to meet your needs!" Nothing can be further from the truth. If you deviate from the optimum asset allocation in any direction, you *are* reducing the longevity of your income portfolio.

Based on each portfolio profile, I determined an optimum asset mix for a range of withdrawal rates. It is not always as clear-cut as it is in Figure 13. Sometimes judgement is needed. Observation a combination of the lowest probability of depletion and the highest minimum and then the average portfolio life is required. You first have to determine at what asset mix the peak minimum portfolio life occurs and then find the minimum depletion for that portfolio life and asset mix. While doing that, it is important to keep the average portfolio life in the forefront: The optimization should be confirmed at the average portfolio life. It does not make sense to optimize the asset mix for 30-years, if the average life of that portfolio profile is only 12 years.

58

I combined the optimum asset allocation in Figure 15, which I called "Optimum Portfolio Topography". The horizontal scale shows the initial withdrawal rate. The vertical scale shows the portfolio life. Knowing the two, you can then read off the optimum equity percentage on the chart. The fixed income portion is the difference between 100% and the optimum equity percentage.

OPTIMUM PORTFOLIO TOPOGRAPHY

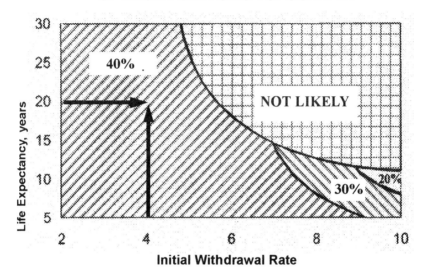

Figure 15. Optimum Portfolio Topography for years 1900-1999. Equity portion of performs the same as the DJIA.

For example, if you are designing a portfolio for a twenty-year life expectancy and a 4% initial withdrawal rate (which is adjusted for inflation over time), draw a vertical line from "4" on the horizontal scale and a horizontal line from "20" on the vertical scale. Where the two lines meet is in the 40% region on the chart. That means your portfolio would include 40% equities and the remaining 60% would be allocated to fixed income. Based on one hundred years of data this mix would give you the lowest probability of depletion and the highest longevity.

If the probability of depletion exceeded 50% then the asset mix becomes irrelevant. This area is marked as "NOT LIKELY" on the chart.

In general, the higher the withdrawal rate the higher the percentage of fixed income in your portfolio. That is because higher withdrawals deplete the portfolio sooner and the equities don't have much time to grow. Lower withdrawals give the portfolio a longer life, not only because less money is withdrawn but also because equities have a longer time to appreciate in value.

Right Shift and Left Shift:

The optimum portfolio topography in Figure 15 is based on the equities in a portfolio performing identically to the DJIA. If the equities in the portfolio outperform the index then the optimum asset mix shifts toward a larger percentage of equities. On the other hand, if equities in the portfolio underperform the index then the optimum asset mix shifts towards a larger percentage of fixed income. This makes sense because if your equities were underperforming the benchmark index why would you want to put more money into them?

Table 2 summarizes the optimum asset mix based on historic data for the strategic asset allocation model in a simplified format:

Table 2: Optimum Asset Mix for Strategic Asset Allocation for an income portfolio rebalanced each year.

Equity Performance Relative to the DJIA	Initial Withdrawal Rate Rate	Optimum Asset Mix Fixed Income %	Equity %
DJIA +4%	3% or less	40	60
	over 3% to 10%	60	40
DJIA +2%	10% or less	60	40
DJIA	9% or less	60	40
	over 9% to 10%	80	20
DJIA –2%	3% or less	60	40
	over 3% to 10%	80	20
DJIA –4%	10% or less	80	20

Optimizing the Rebalancing Method:

Each year many advisors and investors busily rebalance their portfolios. This accomplishes two things:

- It reduces the portfolio volatility,
- It gives the appearance that "something" is being done.

The conventional wisdom is that rebalancing annually reduces volatility of the portfolio. Most advisors that I have met follow this religiously, so much so that in some companies rebalancing is treated as a magic ritual that keeps away most of the evils of fluctuation and the associated risk. Some even rebalance quarterly! If rebalancing frequently is so good for the portfolio, why not rebalance every day! Surely it will give the appearance of doing "something"!

I tried rebalancing at different time intervals, from annually to every ten years and anything in between. For example, here are the life of portfolios if someone who retired in 1929 (a bad year) and someonein 1933 (a good year) with an initial withdrawal rate of 5%. The effects of and rebalancing every four years versus rebalancing each year are compared.

ASSET MIX
(Fixed Income / Equity)

	20 / 80	40 / 60	60 / 40	80 / 20
	PORTFOLIO LIFE (years)			
Retire in 1929:				
Rebalance every year	13.4	17.9	21.7	25.2
Rebalance every four years	14.5	22.4	28.5	29.8
Retire in 1933:				
Rebalance every year	48.6	39.5	28.3	21.9
Rebalance every four years	52.7	45.2	33.3	24.0

Rebalancing every four years improved the portfolio longevity for both 1929 and 1933. Looking at the whole century, rebalancing every four years helped to increase portfolio life in some cases and hampered others.

However, in the final analysis, it did not help increase portfolio life for the whole century.

My next step was to base the rebalancing on market cycles. In Chapter 1, I talked about the market cycles. We also covered the devastating effect of the dollar cost averaging which occurs because of these market cycles in income portfolios.

Periodic Rebalancing based on Market Cycles:

What are cycles? Cycles are patterns which repeat themselves time over time on a regular basis. Some examples are bird migrations, the tides, planetary movements etc. When applied to markets, some of the better-known cycles are:
- 54-year Kondratieff Cycle,
- 18-year cycle,
- 10-year decennial cycle,
- 4-year U.S. presidential cycle,
- 1-year seasonality cycle

The *first rule* of rebalancing is that it reduces the volatility of the cycles of *smaller periodicity only.* If you rebalance each and every year you are basically reducing the volatility of the 1-year seasonality cycle and cycles with smaller lengths. It does very little to help reduce the effects of larger cycles on income portfolios.

If you rebalance more often than the period of the larger cycle, basically what you are doing is averaging down the cost of your equities in falling markets. This will shorten the longevity of an income portfolio as it moves through mega-bear market cycles. For example: If you retired in 1989 in Japan and you were counting on your investment portfolio for income, annual rebalancing certainly reduced the portfolio volatility but it also propelled you to poverty a lot sooner than rebalancing say, every ten years.

Now the second question is: what is the best cycle to use?

The 54-year Kondratieff cycle[15] is far too long for any retirement planning. Also, a large portion of retirees may be dead after 18 years, so the 18-year cycle is out of the question as well.

---

[15] Named after its discoverer, Nikolai D. Kondratieff, a Russian economist. He was sent to Siberian labour camps for his research of capitalistic economies. See his book called "The Long Wave Cycle" translated by Guy Daniels. On the same theme, two other interesting books are "The K Wave" by David Knox, and "The Great Cycle" by Dick Stoken.

The decennial cycle[16] may be useful for retirees who are withdrawing small amounts of income from their portfolio, but it would not work when withdrawal amounts are 4% or higher, because the portfolio would run out of money after one or two rebalancing acts.

The U.S. presidential cycle[17] is well within the time frame of any retirement projection so I tried that as my guide to rebalance my model portfolios. According to the presidential cycle, the stock prices decline following an election. At mid-term the stock prices start rising again until the election year.

Between 1900 and 1999, the average annual growth of the Dow Jones Industrial Average and its standard deviation were as following:

U.S. Presidential Cycle	Average DJIA Growth	Standard Deviation
1st year	6%	23.5%
2nd year	3%	19.9%
3rd year	12%	26.3%
4th year (election year)	10%	19.6%

When I rebalanced income portfolios at the end of each U.S. election year *only*, most portfolios lasted longer and their probability of depletion reduced. Only at high withdrawal rates *and* high equity content in the portfolio, annual rebalancing was more effective than rebalancing based on U.S. Presidential cycle .

In my models, the periodic income is first withdrawn from the cash or fixed income portion of the portfolio. We do that because we have already seen the devastating effects of dollar-cost averaging when withdrawals are taken out of equities. Only if there is insufficient cash, then the income is generated by selling equities. This being the case, could there be situations where it may be better not to rebalance an income portfolio at all?

---

[16] First observed by Edgar Lawrence Smith, author of "Tides and the Affairs of Men" and also his bestseller in the 1920's, "Common Stocks as a Long-Term Investment".

[17] This cycle is also applies to Canadian stock markets as well because of its correlation with the U.S. economy.

The answer is "yes". There are situations where it is better not to rebalance at all. This occurs at low withdrawal rates and in portfolios with a low percentage of equity. It also works well if the portfolio is outperforming the index. This gives equities time to grow more than they would if you were to rebalance periodically.

Here is an example for a portfolio with 80% fixed income and 20% equities outperforming the index by 4%. The initial withdrawal rate is 5%:

	Minimum Portfolio Life	Probability of Depletion after		
		20 years	25 years	30 years
Rebalance each year	17.4 years	8%	20%	30%
Rebalance only on the U.S. election year	18.2 years	6%	11%	26%
Never rebalance	24.3 years	0%	1%	33%

Growth Rebalancing:

So far, we have only looked at rebalancing at regular time intervals. There is another rebalancing technique that is worth mentioning. This technique is based on how much your equities grow each year.

The historic average growth of the Dow Jones Industrial Average (DJIA) is about 8% per year. Instead of rebalancing the portfolio at a fixed time interval, doesn't it make sense that we rebalance *only* if the DJIA grew more than its historic average during the year?

The answer is "yes". In many cases, it makes sense to rebalance only if the equity index grows more than its historic average.

Let's call this strategy "growth rebalancing". Here is how it works: We start our portfolio with our optimum asset allocation. At the end of each year, we look at the growth in the equity benchmark index (DJIA). If it grew more than a "threshold" value then we sell a portion of equities and put this money into fixed income. Otherwise, we leave the portfolio alone and don't rebalance. We only "ring the cash register" if equities are making money.

As it turns out, this optimum threshold value depends on whether the equity portion of our portfolio outperforms or underperforms its underlying index. If the return is the same as the index, then this threshold value worked out to be 12%. If the equity portion of your portfolio underperforms the index (bad funds, high MERs[18]), 10% was the threshold. If the return of the equity portion of your portfolio outperforms the index (good funds, DRIP's), then 15% was the optimum threshold. These numbers gave the longest portfolio life with the lowest risk of depletion for the one hundred years studied.

This makes sense: If our equities are underperforming the index we want to cash them out sooner to provide us with income. If our equities are outperforming the index, we want to hold on to them longer, hence the higher threshold.

The next question is how much of the growth should be taken out for rebalancing. Well, again that depends on your withdrawal rate and whether your equities are outperforming or underperforming the index. If your equities outperform the index then you need to redeem a smaller portion of the growth. As it worked out, this number which I call the "redemption multiplier", varied between one-half and twice the growth rate amount for all combinations and permutations that I studied.

In most cases, the growth rebalancing technique was superior to periodic rebalancing. Here is an example for a portfolio, initially holding 20% in fixed income and 80% in an average equity mutual fund that is expected to underperform the index by 2%. The initial withdrawal rate is 4%:

	Average Portfolio Life	Probability of Depletion after:		
		20 years	25 years	30 years
Rebalance each year	25.5 years	34%	56%	66%
Growth rebalancing	35.2 years	13%	24%	37%

---

[18]   MER is an acronym for "Management Expense Ratio". It is includes the fees and expenses that a mutual fund company charges to its investors. It expressed as percentage of fund value.

In this particular case, the risk of portfolio depletion was reduced by about half by utilizing growth rebalancing compared to annual rebalancing. The average portfolio life increased from 25.5 years to 35.2 years which is a significant improvement.

So we see that there is not a single way of optimum rebalancing for all and every income portfolio. This brings us to the *second rule of rebalancing*: The optimum rebalancing technique depends on the *withdrawal rate* and on the *relative performance of your equities* in your portfolio.

Table 3 summarizes the optimum asset allocation and rebalancing method, portfolio life and probability of depletion. If the optimum rebalancing technique happens to be growth rebalancing, then the "growth threshold" and "redemption multiplier" are shown in parenthesis.

Figure 16 compares the portfolio values after retirement for the *optimized* strategic asset allocation to *standard* strategic asset allocation. Optimizing the strategic asset allocation and the rebalancing method increases the average portfolio life. This is visible in the charts as there are more years with a higher portfolio value when optimum strategic asset allocation is utilized. The workload to care for the portfolio will likely be reduced as well because in a lot of the cases, the rebalancing is needed only every four years on the U.S. Presidential election year.

Table 3: Optimum Asset Allocation and Optimum Rebalancing Method for Strategic Asset Allocation

Equity Performance Relative to DJIA	Initial Withdrawal Rate	Optimum Asset Mix Fixed Income %	Equity %	Optimum Rebalancing Technique	Minimum Portfolio Life years	Average Portfolio Life years	% Probability of Depletion after 10 years	20 years	30 years
DJIA + 4%	3%	40	60	No Rebalancing	40+	40+	0	0	0
	4%	60	40	No Rebalancing	40+	40+	0	0	0
	5%	60	40	Growth (15%, 0.75)	23.0	38.1	0	0	20
	6%	60	40	Growth (15%, 0.75)	17.2	28.8	0	15	63
	8%	60	40	Growth (15%, 0.75)	12.0	18.8	0	63	94
	10%	60	40	Growth (15%, 0.75)	8.9	14.3	10	83	100
DJIA + 2%	3%	60	40	No Rebalancing	40+	40+	0	0	0
	4%	60	40	No Rebalance	29.6	39.6	0	0	3
	5%	60	40	Growth (15%, 1.25)	18.8	32.2	0	1	50
	6%	60	40	Growth (15%, 1.25)	15.2	24.3	0	31	76
	8%	60	40	Growth (15%, 1.00)	11.0	17.1	0	75	99
	10%	60	40	Growth (15%, 1.00)	8.5	13.2	16	93	100
DJIA	3%	60	40	No Rebalancing	38.4	40+	0	0	0
	4%	60	40	US Pr. Election	22.3	37.1	0	0	20
	5%	60	40	US Pr. Election	16.6	29.3	0	11	66
	6%	60	40	US Pr. Election	13.6	24.2	0	45	86
	8%	60	40	US Pr. Election	10.1	16.6	0	78	93
	10%	80	20	US Pr. Election	8.3	12.7	19	93	100
DJIA – 2%	3%	60	40	No Rebalancing	31.6	40+	0	0	0
	4%	80	20	US Pr. Election	19.9	36.2	0	1	21
	5%	80	20	Growth (10%, 2.00)	15.5	27.6	0	18	67
	6%	80	20	Growth (10%, 2.00)	12.9	21.5	0	35	93
	8%	80	20	Growth (10%, 2.00)	9.9	15.5	1	86	100
	10%	80	20	Growth (10%, 2.00)	8.2	12.3	18	100	100
DJIA – 4%	3%	80	20	Growth (10%, 1.50)	26.6	40+	0	0	7
	4%	80	20	Growth (10%, 2.00)	19.2	36.9	0	3	24
	5%	80	20	Growth (10%, 2.00)	15.1	26.9	0	18	73
	6%	80	20	Growth (10%, 2.00)	12.7	21.1	0	43	93
	8%	80	20	Growth (10%, 2.00)	9.7	15.2	1	86	100
	10%	80	20	Growth (10%, 2.00)	8.1	12.1	19	100	100

Figure 16. Portfolio value for retirement years between 1900-1999: Optimized Strategic Asset Allocation and Rebalancing versus the Standard Strategic Asset Allocation (60% fixed income, 40% equity, rebalanced annually). The heavy line is the standard retirement model.

Optimizing the strategic asset mix and rebalancing technique increased the average portfolio life. One can observe that there are more occurrences of larger portfolio values with optimizing.

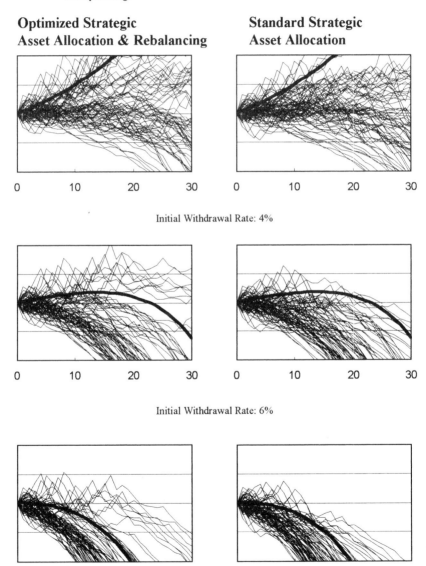

To illustrate the optimum asset allocation and rebalancing, let's look at some examples:

> *Example 1: Bob has $750,000 in his retirement portfolio. He is just retiring. He needs to draw $37,500 income from this portfolio. After the first year this withdrawal amount will be adjusted for inflation. His equities consist of a diversified DRIP portfolio that has been outperforming the DJIA by 4%.*
>
> 1. *Bob's initial withdrawal rate is 5%, calculated as:*
>
> $$\frac{\$37,500}{\$750,000} \ x \ 100\% \ = 5\%$$
>
> 2. *Go to Table 3: For relative equity performance of DJIA +4% and an initial withdrawal rate of 5%, the optimum asset allocation is 40% equity and 60% fixed income. Table 3 shows that for this portfolio during the last century, the minimum and average portfolio life was 23.0 and 38.1 years, respectively. Bob invests 40% of his assets ($300,000) in equities and 60% ($450,000) in fixed income.*
>
> 3. *In Table 3, Bob reads that the optimum rebalancing technique is "Growth Rebalancing". He notes that the growth threshold is 15% and the multiplier is 0.75.*
>
> • *If at the end of the year, the DJIA grew less than 15% for that year, Bob does not rebalance that year. He skips to Step 4.*
>
> • *If at the end of the year, the DJIA grew more than 15% for that year, then Bob figures out the growth of his equity holdings during that year. The redemption multiplier is 0.75, so he multiplies this growth with 0.75. In other words, he redeems 75% of the growth during that year from his equities and invests it in fixed income.*
>
> 4. *At the end of each year he repeats Step 3.*

Example 2: Five years into his retirement, due to a market correction, Bob now has $600,000 in his retirement portfolio. At the same time, he was pleasantly surprised to find out that he was eligible for more pension benefits. Now he needs to draw only $24,000 income from his portfolio. In a further development his brother-in-law talked him into selling his stocks and instead buying a DJIA index fund.

Each time the withdrawal rate or the relative performance of equities changes for any reason other than inflation, the optimum asset mix and rebalancing strategy must be reviewed and recalculated.

In this example, the withdrawal rate changed. Also by liquidating his DRIP portfolio and buying index funds, the relative performance of Bob's equities have changed. Even if only one of these events had occurred Bob had to re-establish his optimum asset mix and rebalancing technique.

1. *Bob's new initial withdrawal rate is 4%, calculated as:*

$$\frac{\$24,000}{\$600,000} \times 100\% = 4\%$$

2. *In Table 3, Bob reads: For relative equity performance of the DJIA and an initial withdrawal rate of 4%, the optimum asset allocation is still the same, i.e. 40% Equity and 60% Fixed income. So there is no need to change the original asset mix. Based on historic data, from this point on, Bob can expect a minimum and average portfolio life of 22.3 and 37.1 years, respectively.*

3. *The optimum rebalancing technique is now different than before. Bob needs to rebalance his portfolio at the end of every U.S. Presidential election year.*

Example 3: *Fifteen years later, Bob's annual withdrawals are $45,000. This amount gives him the same purchasing power as the $24,000 of fifteen years ago. Bob realizes that the inflation was somewhat higher during these fifteen years than the historic average. The market value of his income portfolio value is now $250,000.*

1. *Bob's current withdrawal rate is 18%, calculated as:*

$$\frac{\$45,000}{\$250,000} \times 100\% = 18\%$$

Keep an eye on the current withdrawal rate. Once it is over 12% then withdrawals are excessive relative to the portfolio size. The remaining portfolio life is now predictably shortened.

2. *Because Bob's current withdrawal rate is over 12%, it is considered unsustainable. Using the "remaining portfolio life" equation at the end of Chapter 4 we calculate:*

$$RPL, years = \frac{A}{CWR}$$

A is:
100 for the average remaining portfolio life
150 for the maximum remaining portfolio life
75 for the minimum remaining portfolio life

Bob's remaining portfolio life based on one hundred years of history is then:

Average: 5.5 years (calculated as 100/18)
Maximum: 8.3 years (calculated as 150/18)
Minimum: 4.2 years (calculated as 75/18)

Chapter 6
Reducing the Initial Risk

You have done all your homework. You have established your optimum asset mix. You have studied every detail be they stocks, bonds or mutual funds. Everything is according to your checklist. You are ready to invest all of your money. Now is the time to push the button and implement your plan.

Wait… You read in the paper that the market may crash. One "expert" says, "markets are so low, they can't go any lower!" Another "expert" says: "this is the best buying opportunity!" It seems there are more opinions than people on the planet. What do you do? Whose opinion do you trust?

There is no guarantee that the market won't crash the day after you invest all of your money. It happens. If you are worried about it then instead of implementing your "ideal asset mix" immediately you can gradually work your way into the final asset mix over time.

Let's look at three methods:
- Dollar-Cost averaging,
- Dollar-Cost averaging based on the U.S. Presidential cycle,
- Growth averaging.

Dollar-Cost Averaging

In Chapter 1 we saw the damage dollar-cost averaging can cause for an income portfolio, so why are we still talking about it here? Well, here we use the dollar-cost averaging method to buy equities in our portfolio as opposed to selling, so it is beneficial. Only if we were selling them to generate income would it be damaging.

As usual, we first establish the optimum asset mix. We invest all the money that is allocated to fixed income, fully. As for the equity side, instead of investing the whole amount all at once, we invest ¼ of it each year over four years until the final asset mix is achieved.

Example:

Say we have a portfolio of one million dollars and our optimum asset mix is 60% fixed income and 40% equities.

We invest the 60% of our assets ($600,000) in fixed income, probably in a bond ladder.

Now we have to deal with the 40% ($400,000) allocated to equities. Instead of investing it all at once, we invest only $100,000 (¼ of the allocated amount) into equities. We invest the rest of the money into short-term money market funds. Each year, we take out $100,000 from this money market fund and invest it in equities.

We continue doing that until the optimum asset mix of 60/40 is achieved.

This method reduces the risk during the crucial first four years of retirement. It increases the portfolio life by up to two years.

Table 4 shows the optimum asset allocation and rebalancing method, portfolio life and probability of depletion using dollar-cost averaging.

Figure 17 compares the portfolio values after retirement using dollar-cost averaging with standard strategic asset allocation. The charts clearly show that the volatility is smaller in the earlier years with dollar-cost averaging.

73

Table 4: Optimum Asset Allocation and Optimum Rebalancing Method for Strategic Asset Allocation Dollar-Cost Averaging during the first four years (25% per year)

Equity Performance Relative to the DJIA	Initial Withdrawal Rate	Optimum Asset Mix Fixed Income %	Equity %	Optimum Rebalancing Technique	Minimum Portfolio Life years	Average Portfolio Life years	% Probability of Depletion after: 10 years	20 years	30 years
DJIA + 4%	3%	40	60	No Rebalance	40+	40+	0	0	0
	4%	40	60	US Pr. Election	40+	40+	0	0	0
	5%	40	60	US Pr. Election	22.9	40+	0	0	13
	6%	40	60	US Pr. Election	17.8	28.4	0	11	53
	8%	40	60	Biannual	12.1	19.4	0	66	89
	10%	40	60	Annual	9.0	14.1	9	89	99
DJIA + 2%	3%	40	60	No Rebalance	40+	40+	0	0	0
	4%	60	40	No Rebalance	31.4	39.9	0	0	0
	5%	60	40	US Pr. Election	19.7	31.5	0	1	44
	6%	60	40	US Pr. Election	15.6	24.7	0	31	77
	8%	60	40	US Pr. Election	11.1	18.1	0	74	91
	10%	80	20	Annual	8.6	12.7	17	96	100
DJIA	3%	40	60	US Pr. Election	40+	40+	0	0	0
	4%	60	40	US Pr. Election	23.9	37.6	0	0	17
	5%	60	40	US Pr. Election	17.8	28.4	0	9	69
	6%	60	40	US Pr. Election	14.5	23.5	0	48	87
	8%	60	40	Annual	10.8	15.7	0	88	100
	10%	80	20	Annual	8.6	12.4	19	98	100
DJIA − 2%	3%	60	40	US Pr. Election	30.9	40+	0	0	0
	4%	60	40	US Pr. Election	21.3	33.0	0	0	47
	5%	60	40	US Pr. Election	16.4	26.1	0	19	80
	6%	60	40	US Pr. Election	13.4	21.6	0	49	89
	8%	80	20	Annual	10.3	15.3	1	89	100
	10%	80	20	Annual	8.5	12.2	21	99	100
DJIA − 4%	3%	80	20	Biannual	27.9	40+	0	0	10
	4%	80	20	US Pr. Election	20.0	34.1	0	1	23
	5%	80	20	US Pr. Election	15.6	25.4	0	16	86
	6%	80	20	US Pr. Election	13.1	20.5	0	53	90
	8%	80	20	US Pr. Election	10.0	15.0	1	88	100
	10%	80	20	Annual	8.4	12.0	22	99	100

74

Figure 17. Portfolio value for retirement years between 1900-1999: Dollar-cost averaging of equities in the first four years versus the Standard Strategic Asset Allocation (60% fixed income, 40% equity, rebalanced annually). The heavy line is the standard retirement model.

The dollar-cost averaging method in the early years of the retirement clearly reduced the volatility and increased the minimum portfolio life. However, because it also limits the potential growth in early years it is not as effective in increasing the average portfolio life.

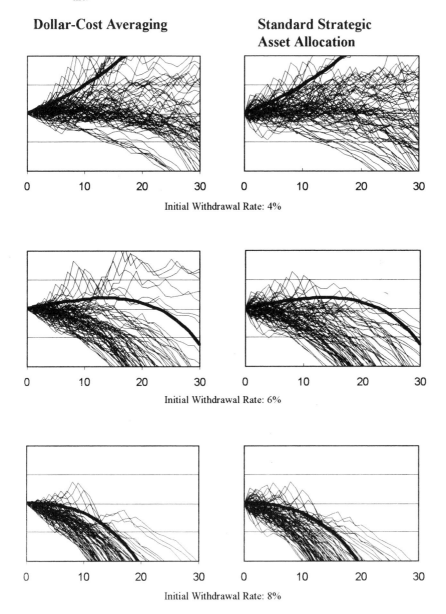

Dollar-Cost Averaging based on the U.S. Presidential Cycle:

Instead of investing 25% annually of the amount that is allocated to equities until the final asset mix is reached, why not vary the percentages to synchronize them with the U.S. Presidential cycle?

As it turned out, investing 10% in the first, third and fourth years and 70% in the second year of the presidential term, achieved the longest portfolio life. Doing so increased the portfolio life by up to two years.

> *Example:*
>
> *Say we have a portfolio of one million dollars and our optimum asset mix is 60% fixed income and 40% equities.*
>
> *We invest the 60% of our assets ($600,000) in fixed income, probably in a bond ladder.*
>
> *Now we have to deal with the 40% ($400,000) allocated to equities.*
>
> *If it is the first, third or fourth year of the U.S. Presidential term then we invest only $40,000 (10% of the allocated amount) into equities. If it is the second year of the U.S. Presidential term then we invest $280,000 (70% of the allocated amount) into equities. We invest the rest of the money into short-term money market funds*
>
> *Each year, using the same logic, we take the appropriate amount (depending on which year of the U.S. Presidential term it is) from this money market fund and invest it into equities.*
>
> *We continue doing that until the optimum asset mix of 60/40 is reached.*

Table 5 shows the optimum asset allocation and rebalancing method, portfolio life and probability of depletion using this method.

Figure 18 compares the portfolio values after retirement using this method with the standard strategic asset allocation.

Table 5: Optimum Asset Allocation and Optimum Rebalancing Method for Strategic Asset Allocation Dollar-Cost Averaging during the first four years based on the U.S. Presidential election cycle (10% at the end of the first, third and fourth years, 70% at the end of the second year of the presidential term)

Equity Performance Relative to the DJIA	Initial Withdrawal Rate	Optimum Asset Mix		Optimum Rebalancing Technique	Minimum Portfolio Life years	Average Portfolio Life years	Probability of Depletion after:		
		Fixed Income %	Equity %				10 years	20 years	30 years
DJIA + 4%	3%	60	40	US Pr. Election	40+	40+	0	0	0
	4%	60	40	US Pr. Election	38.1	40+	0	0	0
	5%	60	40	US Pr. Election	24.4	36.0	0	0	20
	6%	60	40	US Pr. Election	18.1	26.5	0	15	69
	8%	40	60	Annual	12.5	20.1	0	65	91
	10%	40	60	Annual	9.6	14.2	7	86	99
DJIA + 2%	3%	40	60	US Pr. Election	40+	40+	0	0	0
	4%	60	40	US Pr. Election	30.2	40+	0	0	0
	5%	60	40	US Pr. Election	21.3	32.2	0	0	46
	6%	60	40	US Pr. Election	16.3	23.9	0	35	76
	8%	60	40	US Pr. Election	11.4	18.1	0	75	91
	10%	60	40	Annual	9.0	12.8	17	95	100
DJIA	3%	60	40	US Pr. Election	39.5	40+	0	0	0
	4%	60	40	US Pr. Election	25.5	36.9	0	0	20
	5%	60	40	US Pr. Election	18.8	27.7	0	9	69
	6%	60	40	US Pr. Election	15.0	23.7	0	51	87
	8%	60	40	Annual	11.2	15.7	0	85	99
	10%	80	20	Annual	8.6	12.4	18	98	100
DJIA − 2%	3%	60	40	US Pr. Election	33.0	40+	0	0	0
	4%	60	40	US Pr. Election	22.6	33.1	0	0	43
	5%	60	40	US Pr. Election	16.7	26.2	0	20	79
	6%	60	40	US Pr. Election	13.9	21.2	0	58	87
	8%	60	40	Annual	10.6	14.8	0	91	100
	10%	80	20	Annual	8.5	12.2	21	98	100
DJIA − 4%	3%	80	20	No Rebalancing	29.2	40+	0	0	9
	4%	80	20	Bi-annual	20.4	33.4	0	0	26
	5%	80	20	US Pr. Election	16.0	25.4	0	18	86
	6%	80	20	US Pr. Election	13.3	20.5	0	55	91

Figure 18. Portfolio value for retirement years between 1900-1999: Dollar-Cost Averaging based on the U.S. Presidential cycle versus the Standard Strategic Asset Allocation (60% fixed income, 40% equity, rebalanced annually). The heavy line is the standard retirement model.

The volatility is less in the early years of retirement with dollar-cost averaging using the U.S. Presidential cycle. The minimum portfolio life is also increased because of reduced losses in the early years of retirement. There are also more years which produced higher portfolio values.

Dollar-Cost Averaging based on the U.S. Presidential Cycle   Standard Strategic Asset Allocation

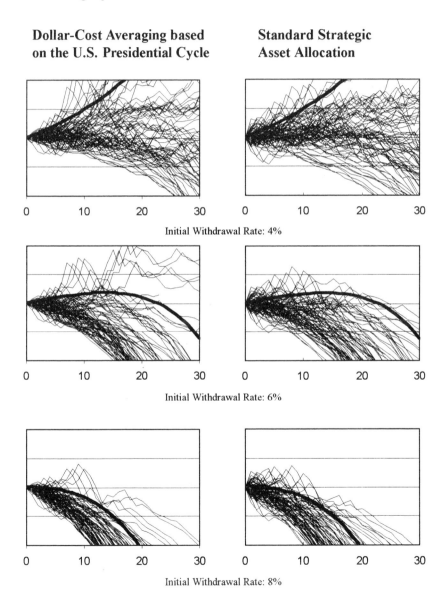

Initial Withdrawal Rate: 4%

Initial Withdrawal Rate: 6%

Initial Withdrawal Rate: 8%

Growth Averaging:

The dollar-cost averaging and U.S. Presidential cycle methods are based on investing certain dollar amounts each year. On the other hand, growth averaging is based on adding to your equity investments only in rising markets. There is no specific time period.

How does growth averaging work? We first determine our optimum asset mix. Say it is 60% fixed income and 40% equities. At the start, instead of investing all of the 40% into equity, we invest only 10%. We keep the rest, 30%, in the money market. When and if the value of our equities increase by 15%, we transfer 10% of the portfolio value from the money market fund to equities[19]. We continue doing that until our asset mix reaches 60% fixed income and 40% equity. After that point, the portfolio reverts to the optimum rebalancing process.

Example:

Say we have a portfolio of one million dollars and our optimum asset mix is 60% fixed income and 40% equities.

We invest 60% of our assets ($600,000) in fixed income, probably in a bond ladder.

Now we have to deal with the 40% ($400,000) allocated to equities.

In the first year we invest only $100,000 (10% of the portfolio value) into equities. We invest the rest of the money into short-term money market funds. At this point our asset mix is 10% equities and 90% cash/fixed income.

We wait until the value of our equities increase by $15,000 (15% of $100,000 invested into equities) to $115,000. It may happen in a few months, or it may happen in a few years. Let's say that whenever that happens our portfolio is worth $900,000. Because our equity holdings are still below 40%, we transfer another $90,000 (10% of the portfolio

---

[19] The initial investment amount of 10%, and subsequent additions of 10% after a 15% growth, are not arbitrary numbers; they are the optimum numbers for the time period 1900-1999.

value) from the money market fund into equities. Now we have $205,000 in equities. At this point our asset mix is 22.8% equities and 77.2% cash/ fixed income.

We wait until the value of our equities increase by $30,750 (15% of $205,000 invested into equities) to $235,750. When that occurs, let's say our portfolio is worth $930,000. Because our equity holdings are still below 40%, we transfer another $93,000 (10% of the portfolio value) from the money market fund into equities. Now we have $328,750 in equities. At this point our asset mix is 35.3% equities and 64.7% cash/fixed income.

We wait until the value of our equities increases by $49,313 (15% of $328,750 invested into equities) to $378,063. Whenever that occurs, let's say at that point our portfolio is worth $890,000. Now, our equity holdings are 42%. That means we have already reached our optimum asset mix.

As soon as we reach our optimum asset mix, the growth averaging method is finished. From this point on, we carry on with the optimum rebalancing process as shown on Table 6.

Growth averaging does not significantly increase the minimum and average portfolio life for the entire study period however, it minimizes the devastating effect of retiring just at the beginning of a bear market. It follows a more predictable path. No money is added to the equities during a bear market. If the bear market turns bullish, you still have plenty of cash to take advantage of the situation.

Table 6 shows the optimum asset allocation and rebalancing method, portfolio life and probability of depletion using this method.

Figure 19 compares the portfolio values for the growth averaging method to the standard strategic asset allocation method.

Table 6: Optimum Asset Allocation and Optimum Rebalancing Method for Strategic Asset Allocation when the Growth Averaging technique is used to reduce the initial risk.

Equity Performance Relative to the DJIA	Initial Withdrawal Rate	Optimum Asset Mix Fixed Income %	Equity %	Optimum Rebalancing Technique	Minimum Portfolio Life years	Average Portfolio Life years	Probability of Depletion after: 10 years	20 years	30 years
DJIA + 4%	3%	40	60	No Rebalancing	40+	40+	0	0	0
	4%	40	60	No Rebalancing	40+	40+	0	0	0
	5%	40	60	US Pr. Election	23.0	35.7	0	0	26
	6%	20	80	US Pr. Election	16.6	25.4	0	19	64
	8%	20	80	Annual	10.8	18.3	0	75	96
	10%	60	40	Annual	8.7	13.1	17	96	100
DJIA + 2%	3%	40	60	No Rebalancing	40+	40+	0	0	0
	4%	40	60	US Pr. Election	27.2	40+	0	0	6
	5%	40	60	US Pr. Election	19.9	30.2	0	3	53
	6%	60	40	US Pr. Election	14.7	23.6	0	40	80
	8%	60	40	US Pr. Election	10.3	17.2	0	84	93
	10%	60	40	Annual	8.5	12.5	19	96	100
DJIA	3%	50	50	US Pr. Election	35.8	40+	0	0	0
	4%	50	50	US Pr. Election	22.6	36.3	0	0	24
	5%	50	50	US Pr. Election	17.4	27.6	0	12	74
	6%	50	50	US Pr. Election	13.8	22.8	0	43	90
	8%	80	20	US Pr. Election	10.1	15.9	0	85	97
	10%	80	20	Annual	8.4	12.3	18	99	100
DJIA – 2%	3%	60	40	US Pr. Election	30.5	40+	0	0	0
	4%	60	40	US Pr. Election	21.0	33.9	0	0	40
	5%	60	40	US Pr. Election	16.0	26.1	0	15	86
	6%	80	20	US Pr. Election	13.1	21.5	0	45	89
	8%	80	20	US Pr. Election	10.0	15.5	0	88	100
	10%	80	20	Annual	8.3	12.1	22	100	100
DJIA – 4%	3%	80	20	US Pr. Election	27.2	40+	0	0	10
	4%	80	20	US Pr. Election	19.6	34.5	0	3	24
	5%	80	20	US Pr. Election	15.4	26.0	0	18	86
	6%	80	20	US Pr. Election	12.8	20.8	0	48	90
	8%	80	20	US Pr. Election	9.8	15.1	1	89	100
	10%	80	20	US Pr. Election	8.2	12.1	21	98	100

Figure 19. Portfolio value for retirement years between 1900-1999: Growth Averaging versus the Standard Strategic Asset Allocation (60% fixed income, 40% equity, rebalanced annually). The heavy line is the standard retirement model.

As with the previous methods of reducing the initial risk, growth averaging reduces the volatility in the early years. This increases the minimum portfolio life somewhat but not significantly. It does not increase the average portfolio life because it may miss any bull markets in the early years of retirement.

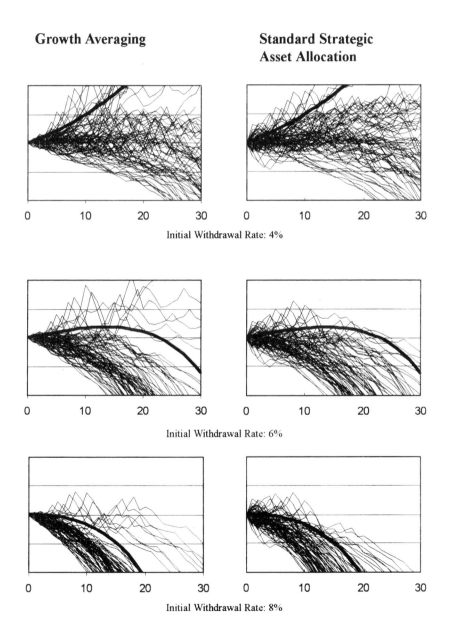

Growth Averaging

Standard Strategic Asset Allocation

Initial Withdrawal Rate: 4%

Initial Withdrawal Rate: 6%

Initial Withdrawal Rate: 8%

The Difference between the Three Methods:

These three methods work to reduce the volatility in the early years and increase the minimum portfolio life. However, it is important to emphasize the fundamental difference between them:

- The Dollar-Cost Averaging is a mechanical system. It does not anticipate any market action. By just investing equal amounts, it reduces the volatility over the first four years of your retirement.

- Using the Dollar-Cost Averaging based on the U. S. Presidential Election cycle **leads** the market action. It reduces the volatility based on its memory of historic data of the U. S. Presidential cycle. Of the three methods, it gives the best improvement to the minimum portfolio life. However, keep in mind that if this cycle manifests itself differently in the future the results may not be as favourable. Therefore, it may not be as reliable.

- The Growth Averaging method **lags** behind the market action. The market has to move up before triggering the next instalment of investment into equities. Because it is lagging behind the markets, of the three methods it gives the least improvement to the minimum portfolio life. However, because it does not count on the memory of cycles, it may be more reliable than the other methods. It prevents your investing heavily in equities in long bear markets regardless of the market history or the cycle theory.

You have to decide for yourself which method best suits your needs and personality, and then stick with it.

Chapter 7

Years of Cash Method

Some investors put aside enough cash (or fixed income) to meet their income needs for a specific number of years. They invest the remainder in equities so there is no specific asset mix. We'll call this "Years of Cash" (YOC) method.

If in any year the cash reserve is below the specific number of years and the value of the equities is higher than a year ago, the growth is used to replenish the cash. Otherwise there is no action.

The income is taken out of the cash portion of the portfolio. If for some reason there is no cash left (usually after a long bear market) then part of the equities are sold to raise the necessary income.

I studied the YOC technique for all the years between 1900 and 1999. I analyzed holding 0, 2, 4, 6, 8, and 10 years of cash. For each year of cash the portfolio life increased by about six to ten months when compared with an all equity portfolio. Table 7 shows the optimum years of cash, portfolio life and probability of depletion using the YOC method.

The YOC method was inferior in most cases when compared with a portfolio based on an optimum strategic asset allocation. The YOC technique forced you to have too much or too little equity in your portfolio in the beginning, depending on your withdrawal rate and it had too much cash towards the end, in all cases.

At low withdrawal rates, the portfolio is more heavily weighted in equities, so it has higher volatility than a strategic asset allocation but not as high as an all-equity portfolio. At higher withdrawal rates, the portfolio is more heavily weighted towards fixed income, so it has lower volatility than a strategic asset allocation but not as low as an all-fixed income portfolio. Figure 20 compares the portfolio values for the YOC method with standard strategic asset allocation.

It seemed to work well only if the equity side significantly outperformed the index for long periods of time. Even then, if you used any one of the three methods of reducing the initial risk (Dollar-cost averaging, the U.S. Presidential cycle, or growth averaging) with an optimum asset mix, you would be better off than using the YOC method.

Table 7: Years of Cash Method

Equity Performance Relative to the DJIA	Initial With-drawal Rate	Optimum Years of Cash	Minimum Portfolio Life years	Average Portfolio Life years	Probability of Depletion after:		
					10 years	20 years	30 years
DJIA + 4%	3%	10	40+	40+	0%	0%	0%
	4%	10	34.0	40+	0%	0%	0%
	5%	10	22.8	35.2	0%	0%	23%
	6%	8	17.0	27.4	0%	15%	57%
	8%	6	11.0	17.0	0%	60%	89%
	10%	6	9.0	13.9	8%	93%	100%
DJIA + 2%	3%	10	38.3	40+	0%	0%	0%
	4%	10	25.2	39.2	0%	0%	7%
	5%	10	19.1	31.1	0%	1%	50%
	6%	10	15.0	24.5	0%	34%	76%
	8%	6	11.0	17.0	0%	75%	100%
	10%	8	8.5	12.7	14%	98%	100%
DJIA	3%	10	27.9	40+	0%	0%	3%
	4%	10	21.7	35.4	0%	0%	30%
	5%	10	16.7	27.1	0%	13%	69%
	6%	10	13.9	21.5	0%	44%	93%
	8%	10	10.2	15.7	0%	89%	100%
	10%	8	8.4	12.3	19%	99%	100%
DJIA − 2%	3%	10	23.3	37.7	0%	0%	17%
	4%	10	18.6	29.3	0%	4%	59%
	5%	10	15.2	23.4	0%	29%	84%
	6%	10	12.8	19.8	0%	58%	97%
	8%	10	9.8	15.2	1%	89%	100%
	10%	10	8.3	12.4	18%	99%	100%
DJIA − 4%	3%	10	20.7	31.1	0%	0%	50%
	4%	10	16.5	24.9	0%	16%	77%
	5%	10	14.1	21.2	0%	45%	97%
	6%	10	12.1	18.4	0%	70%	100%
	8%	10	9.6	14.7	2%	89%	100%
	10%	10	8.3	12.4	18%	99%	100%

Figure 20. Portfolio value for retirement years between 1900-1999: Years-of-Cash method versus the Standard Strategic Asset Allocation (60% fixed income, 40% equity, rebalanced annually). The heavy line is the standard retirement model.

At lower initial withdrawal rates, the YOC method is more volatile than standard strategic asset allocation. At higher withdrawal rates, it is the opposite. Th e YOC method has no significant benefit over the standard strategic asset allocation.

Years of Cash Method   **Standard Strategic Asset Allocation**

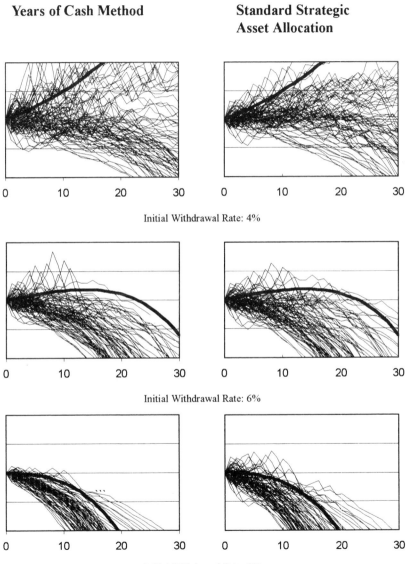

Initial Withdrawal Rate: 4%

Initial Withdrawal Rate: 6%

Initial Withdrawal Rate: 8%

Chapter 8

Measuring Added Value

So far we looked at the following methods:

- Standard strategic asset allocation with annual rebalancing
- Optimized strategic asset allocation with optimized rebalancing
- Years of Cash Method

We also looked at methods of reducing the initial risk by combining the optimized strategic asset allocation/rebalancing with:

- Dollar-cost-averaging
- Dollar-cost averaging in-synch with the U.S. Presidential cycle
- Growth Averaging

All of these methods involve some degree of work. You need to determine your optimum asset mix, follow the portfolio growth and rebalance your portfolio.

Is it really worth spending all that time and effort? How much more life do we add using any one of these methods? How much value do we add?

When we analyse the results, we see that the strategic asset allocation does not always give you the longest possible portfolio life. When we look at the individual years as depicted in Figure 21, it appears that the strategic asset allocation method reduced the portfolio life when compared to either fixed income or equity for someone retiring in 1929, 1933, or 1966. Why then do we use strategic asset allocation?

We use any method or any strategy in retirement planning if it adds value in any one of the following two different ways:

- Increases the *minimum* portfolio life because we don't want to go broke too soon.

- Increases the *average* portfolio life because we want to stretch the portfolio life as long as possible.

In the final analysis, the strategic asset allocation gives you an optimum portfolio life based on one hundred years of history.

Figure 21. Portfolio value when retiring at the beginning of 1929, 1933 and 1966. The initial withdrawal rate is 6% in each case.

If you were counting on your equity investments to provide you with income, both 1929 and 1966 were bad years to retire. You would have been better off investing in fixed income.

If you were counting on your equity investments to provide you with income, 1933 was a good year to retire. Investing in fixed income shortened the longevity of your portfolio.

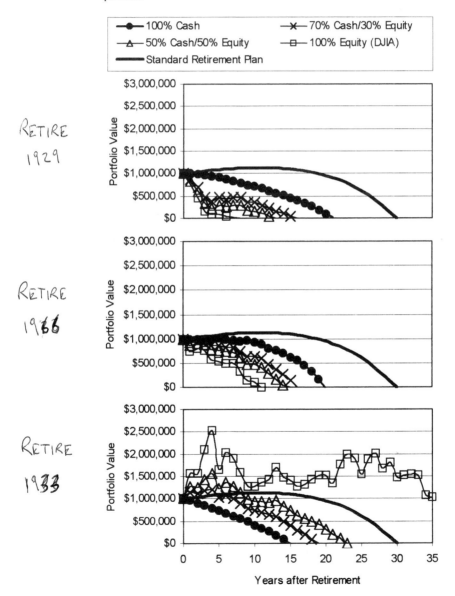

Usually, when you increase the minimum portfolio life you will also be increasing the average portfolio life. But it is not always so. By being more conservative in the early years of the portfolio you may increase the minimum portfolio life but at the same time you may decrease its average life because you may have missed a good bull market in the beginning.

The opposite is also true: Increasing the average portfolio life usually increases the minimum portfolio life, but not always. For example, having your equities outperform the index by 4% adds several years to the average life of your portfolio. However, it is of little help when the markets decline as quickly as they did after the 1929 market crash. Making an extra 4% over the long term does not help much when markets lose 90% within a 3-year period.

So we need to measure the added value separately for both the *minimum* and *average* portfolio life.

We define the "Added Value" as the percentage improvement in portfolio life when compared to a base case. The following pages show the added value for each of the methods and strategies we looked at in previous chapters. In all cases, the equity side is assumed to perform the same as the DJIA.

Standard Strategic Asset Allocation versus All Equity:

The standard Strategic[20] asset allocation improved the portfolio longevity significantly when compared with a 100% equity portfolio. It increased the *minimum* life of the income portfolio. It also increased the *average* portfolio life, especially at lower withdrawal rates. The tables shown here are for an asset mix of 60% fixed income and 40% equity, rebalanced annually.

Standard strategic asset allocation is very important for both the minimum and average life of your income portfolio. Furthermore, it only requires couple of hours of homework each year. Therefore, it should be adhered to for *all* income portfolios. Any variations of asset allocation (optimizing the asset mix, optimizing the rebalancing method, reducing the initial risk) are only there to improve this basic premise.

Added Value – **Minimum** Portfolio Life, 1900-1999:

Initial Withdrawal Rate	Minimum Portfolio Life for Standard Asset Allocation & Annual Rebalancing (years)	Minimum Portfolio Life for 100% Equity (years)	Added Value
4%	21.9	12.1	81%
6%	13.4	7.2	86%
8%	10.0	4.7	112%
10%	8.2	3.7	122%

Added Value – **Average** Portfolio Life, 1900-1999:

Initial Withdrawal Rate	Average Portfolio Life for Standard Asset Allocation & Annual Rebalancing (years)	Average Portfolio Life for 100% Equity (years)	Added Value
4%	37.2	28.7	30%
6%	21.9	19.2	14%
8%	15.7	14.4	9%
10%	12.3	11.5	7%

---

[20] Throughout this book, the Standard Asset Allocation means the conventional, non-optimized asset mix that is rebalanced annually.

Standard Strategic Asset Allocation versus All Fixed Income:

The standard Strategic Asset Allocation added some value when compared with a 100% fixed income portfolio by increasing the *minimum* life of the portfolio, especially at lower withdrawal rates. At higher withdrawal rates where the portfolio life is shorter, the standard strategic asset allocation with annual rebalancing did not add any value.

Standard strategic asset allocation with annual rebalancing did not increase the *average* life when compared to an all-fixed income portfolio.

Added Value – **Minimum** Portfolio Life, 1900-1999:

Initial Withdrawal Rate	Minimum Portfolio Life for Standard Asset Allocation & Annual Rebalancing (years)	Minimum Portfolio Life for 100% Fixed Income (years)	100 Y. STOCKS	Added Value
4%	21.9	19.3	12.1	13%
6%	13.4	12.9	7.2	4%
8%	10.0	10.1	4.7	-1%
10%	8.2	8.3	3.7	-1%

Added Value – **Average** Portfolio Life, 1900-1999:

Initial Withdrawal Rate	Average Portfolio Life for Standard Asset Allocation & Annual Rebalancing (years)	Average Portfolio Life for 100% Fixed Income (years)	100 Y. STOCKS	Added Value
4%	37.2	37.1	28.7	0%
6%	21.9	21.7	19.2	1%
8%	15.7	15.6	14.4	1%
10%	12.3	12.4	11.5	-1%

Optimized versus Standard Asset Allocation:

When we optimize the strategic asset allocation and the corresponding rebalancing method (see Chapter 5, Table 3), we add some value to the *average* life of the portfolio. Normally, this small degree of improvement would not be too interesting. However, considering we had to rebalance most of these portfolios only once every four years on the U.S. Presidential election year instead of every year, it is worth pursuing. Basically, we are getting better results by doing less.

Added Value – **Minimum** Portfolio Life, 1900-1999:

Initial Withdrawal Rate	Minimum Portfolio Life for Optimized Strategic Asset Allocation & Rebalancing (years)	Minimum Portfolio Life for Standard Strategic Asset Allocation & Annual Rebalancing (years)	Added Value
4%	22.3	21.9	2%
6%	13.6	13.4	2%
8%	10.1	10.0	1%
10%	8.3	8.2	1%

Added Value – **Average** Portfolio Life, 1900-1999:

Initial Withdrawal Rate	Average Portfolio Life for Optimized Strategic Asset Allocation & Rebalancing (years)	Average Portfolio Life for Standard Strategic Asset Allocation & Annual Rebalancing (years)	Added Value
4%	37.1	37.2	0%
6%	24.2	21.9	10%
8%	16.6	15.7	6%
10%	12.7	12.3	3%

Years of Cash Method versus Standard Strategic Asset Allocation:

The Years of Cash method tries to give the investor a sense of security by putting aside sufficient cash to meet the investor's income needs for a certain number of years.

The historic data shows that this technique is not better than the standard strategic asset allocation method.

If equities in the portfolio were outperforming the index by 4% annually, then the years of cash method was somewhat better than the standard strategic asset allocation. Even then, it was still inferior to the optimized strategic asset allocation and rebalancing, as we demonstrated in Chapter 7.

Added Value – **Minimum** Portfolio Life, 1900-1999:

Initial Withdrawal Rate	Minimum Portfolio Life for Years of Cash Method (years)	Minimum Portfolio Life for Standard Strategic Asset Allocation & Annual Rebalancing (years)	Added Value
4%	21.7	21.9	-1%
6%	13.9	13.4	4%
8%	10.2	10.0	2%
10%	8.4	8.2	2%

Added Value – **Average** Portfolio Life, 1900-1999:

Initial Withdrawal Rate	Average Portfolio Life for Years of Cash Method (years)	Average Portfolio Life for Standard Strategic Asset Allocation & Annual Rebalancing (years)	Added Value
4%	35.4	37.2	-5%
6%	21.5	21.9	-2%
8%	15.7	15.7	0%
10%	12.3	12.3	0%

Reducing the Initial Risk by Dollar-Cost Averaging versus Standard Strategic Asset Allocation:

The equity risk can be reduced in the early years by dollar-cost averaging into equities over four years, as opposed to investing all at once.

Dollar-cost averaging increases the *minimum* portfolio life. However, because it also limits the potential growth in early years, it is not as effective in increasing the *average* portfolio life.

Added Value – **Minimum** Portfolio Life, 1900-1999:

Initial Withdrawal Rate	Minimum Portfolio Life for Dollar-Cost Averaging & Optimized Strategic Asset Allocation and Rebalancing (years)	Minimum Portfolio Life for Standard Strategic Asset Allocation & Annual Rebalancing (years)	Added Value
4%	23.9	21.9	9%
6%	14.5	13.4	8%
8%	10.8	10.0	8%
10%	8.6	8.2	5%

Added Value – **Average** Portfolio Life, 1900-1999:

Initial Withdrawal Rate	Average Portfolio Life for Dollar-Cost Averaging & Optimized Strategic Asset Allocation and Rebalancing (years)	Average Portfolio Life for Standard Strategic Asset Allocation & Annual Rebalancing (years)	Added Value
4%	37.6	37.2	1%
6%	23.5	21.9	7%
8%	15.7	15.7	0%
10%	12.4	12.3	1%

**Reducing the Initial Risk by Dollar-Cost Averaging based on U.S.
Presidential Election Cycle versus
Standard Strategic Asset Allocation:**

The equity risk can be reduced in the early years by dollar-cost averaging
based on the U.S. Presidential cycle as opposed to investing all at once.
Ten percent is invested in equities in the first, third and fourth years,
and 70% is invested in the second year of the presidential term.

Dollar-cost averaging increases the *minimum* portfolio life however,
because it also limits the potential growth (and losses) in the early years,
it is not as effective in increasing the *average* portfolio life.

The dollar-cost averaging based on the U.S. Presidential Election Cycle,
is the most effective technique among the three methods cited in this
book to reduce the equity risk in the early years of retirement.

Added Value – **Minimum** Portfolio Life, 1900-1999:

Initial Withdrawal Rate	Minimum Portfolio Life for Dollar-Cost Averaging based on the U.S. Presidential Cycle and Optimized Strategic Asset Allocation and Rebalancing (years)	Minimum Portfolio Life for Standard Strategic Asset Allocation & Annual Rebalancing (years)	Added Value
4%	25.5	21.9	16%
6%	15.0	13.4	12%
8%	11.2	10.0	12%
10%	8.6	8.2	5%

Added Value – **Average** Portfolio Life, 1900-1999:

Initial Withdrawal Rate	Average Portfolio Life for Dollar-Cost Averaging based on the U.S. Presidential Cycle and Optimized Strategic Asset Allocation and Rebalancing (years)	Average Portfolio Life for Standard Strategic Asset Allocation & Annual Rebalancing (years)	Added Value
4%	36.9	37.2	-1%
6%	23.7	21.9	8%
8%	15.7	15.7	0%
10%	12.4	12.3	1%

Reducing the Initial Risk by Growth Averaging versus Standard Strategic Asset Allocation:

The equity risk can be reduced in the early years by growth averaging. Initially, only 10% is invested in equities. Subsequently, each time the equity investment goes up by 15%, another 10% is added to equities until the optimum asset mix is achieved.

Growth averaging does not increase the *minimum* or *average* portfolio life significantly, it just makes it more predictable. It may be suitable for investors who want more stability in their portfolios in the early years of their retirement. Other than that, it does not add much value.

Added Value – **Minimum** Portfolio Life, 1900-1999:

Initial Withdrawal Rate	Minimum Portfolio Life for Growth Averaging & Optimized Strategic Asset Allocation and Rebalancing (years)	Minimum Portfolio Life for Standard Strategic Asset Allocation & Annual Rebalancing (years)	Added Value
4%	22.6	21.9	3%
6%	13.8	13.4	3%
8%	10.1	10.0	1%
10%	8.4	8.2	2%

Added Value – **Average** Portfolio Life, 1900-1999:

Initial Withdrawal Rate	Average Portfolio Life for Growth Averaging & Optimized Strategic Asset Allocation and Rebalancing (years)	Average Portfolio Life for Standard Strategic Asset Allocation & Annual Rebalancing (years)	Added Value
4%	36.3	37.2	-2%
6%	22.8	21.9	4%
8%	15.9	15.7	1%
10%	12.3	12.3	0%

Improved Equity Performance:

Historic data shows that an average mutual fund underperforms the index by about 2% a year. While 2% is not a large number in itself, when compounded over time it can make a significant difference to the portfolio life. Keep in mind that it does take more homework but it can add many years to your financial health.

Figure 22 compares the portfolio values after retirement between 1900 and 1999 for the two scenarios. Both portfolios are based on optimized strategic asset allocation & rebalancing based on Table 3 in Chapter 5. At low withdrawal rates, the equities have a longer time to compound and they have a greater impact on the minimum portfolio life.

Added Value – **Minimum** Portfolio Life, 1900-1999:

Initial Withdrawal Rate	Minimum Portfolio Life for DJIA +2% (years)	Minimum Portfolio Life for DJIA -2% (years)	Added Value
4%	29.6	19.9	48%
6%	15.2	12.9	18%
8%	11.0	9.9	11%
10%	8.5	8.2	4%

Added Value – **Average** Portfolio Life, 1900-1999:

Initial Withdrawal Rate	Average Portfolio Life for DJIA +2% (years)	Average Portfolio Life for DJIA -2% (years)	Added Value
4%	39.6	36.2	9%
6%	24.3	21.5	13%
8%	17.1	15.5	10%
10%	13.2	12.3	7%

Figure 22. Portfolio value for retirement years between 1900-1999: Equities outperforming the DJIA by 2% per year versus underperforming the DJIA by 2% per year. The heavy line is the standard retirement model.

Note the increased minimum portfolio life, especially for small withdrawal rates when the equity portfolios outperform the DJIA. Also note larger portfolio values.

DJIA +2%   DJIA -2%

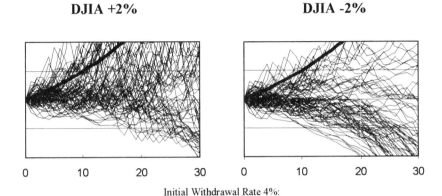

Initial Withdrawal Rate 4%:

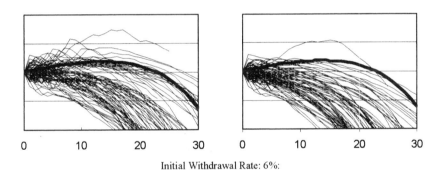

Initial Withdrawal Rate: 6%:

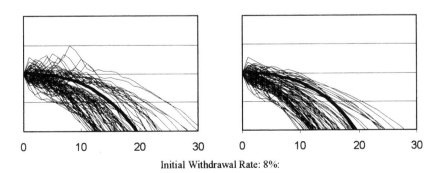

Initial Withdrawal Rate: 8%:

Actively Tracking Equity Investments:

The next step to improving equity performance is actively tracking equity investments. By following the best of mutual funds, holding them only when they are outperforming the index and protecting your portfolio against market crashes, you may be able to beat the index by a wider margin. You may have to spend a few hours a month on your homework. The next chapter, chapter 9, deals with this issue.

In some cases, you don't even need to be active in tracking your equities. During the last 10 years, my Dividend Reinvestment Plan[21] (DRIP) portfolio, consisting of stocks paying high dividends, has been outperforming the underlying index by about 4% a year.

Figure 23 compares the portfolio values for the two scenarios. Both portfolios are based on optimized strategic asset allocation and rebalancingbased on Table 3 in Chapter 5. You can see how actively tracking your equities makes a very large contribution to both the minimum and average life of your income portfolio.

Added Value – **Minimum** Portfolio Life, 1900-1999:

Initial Withdrawal Rate	Minimum Portfolio Life for DJIA +4% (years)	Minimum Portfolio Life for DJIA -2% (years)	Added Value
4%	54.8	19.9	175%
6%	17.2	12.9	154%
8%	12.0	9.9	21%
10%	8.9	8.2	9%

Added Value – **Average** Portfolio Life, 1900-1999:

Initial Withdrawal Rate	Average Portfolio Life for DJIA +4% (years)	Average Portfolio Life for DJIA -2% (years)	Added Value
4%	69.4	36.2	92%
6%	28.8	21.5	34%
8%	18.8	15.5	21%
10%	14.3	12.3	16%

---

[21] See "Commission Free Investing – Handbook of Canadian DRIPs and SPPs" by this author.

Figure 23. Portfolio value for retirement years between 1900-1999: Equities outperforming the DJIA by 4% per year versus underperforming the DJIA by 2% per year. The heavy line is the standard retirement model.

The charts in the left column, where equities outperform DJIA significantly, appear to be more in line with the projections of standard financial plans. Notice how the minimum and the average portfolio life improved significantly.

DJIA +4%　　　　　DJIA -2%

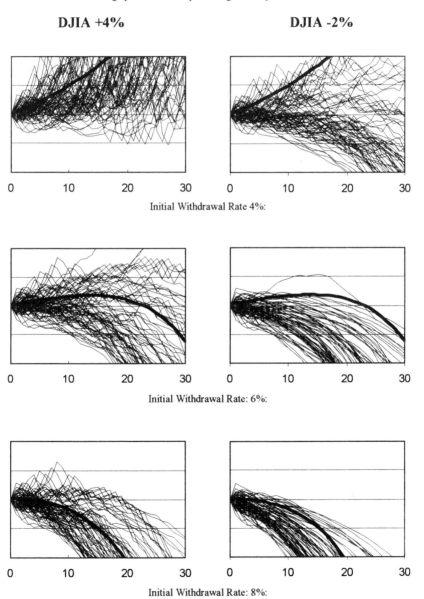

Chapter 9

Fingerprinting Your Mutual Funds

So far, we have only looked at history. We optimized the strategic asset allocation, we optimized the rebalancing techniques and we reduced the equity risk in the early years of retirement. We also reviewed how much value each of these techniques adds to an income portfolio.

In this chapter we look beyond that: I introduce a technique that may help to improve your returns beyond an index's return.

Active versus Passive:

In 1952, Harry Markowitz published[22] his modern portfolio theory (MPT). He tried to create the perfect portfolio by analysing the risk and return of each individual investment. His portfolios included investments that were on the "efficient frontier" of the risk-return curve. This is called active investing.

Towards the end of the mega-bull market of 1949-1962, Mr. Sharpe developed his Capital Asset Pricing Model (CAPM), which seemingly made life easier for investors. With the CAPM, you did not need to analyse individual stocks. CAPM claims that buying the index gives better returns than active portfolio management over the long term. This is called passive investing.

History repeats itself. The index funds found favour again towards the end of the 1982-2000 mega-bull market. Lazy money found its way into passive funds as the bull-run peaked. Subsequently, many investors found out the hard way that buying the index was not such a good idea during bear or sideways markets.

Some actively managed funds follow a style such as value, growth, momentum, contrarian, or sector rotation. Others have no style at all. Regardless, each fund manager convincingly claims that he/she can beat the market over the long term. In fact, less than 20% beat the index at any given time.

The proponents of index funds try to convince you that since only a small portion of the active managers beat the index, why not buy the

---

whole market, i.e. the index? To me this sounds like, "since only a small number of scientists find a cure for a disease, why bother looking for a cure at all?" Just remember this: If you invested $100,000 into the Dow Jones Industrial Average in 1965 and kept it till 1982, your investment would have grown to $107,973. During the same time period, $100,000 invested in the Templeton Growth fund would have become $1,400,235. Which one would you choose?

I don't believe that an active fund manager can beat the index consistently over the long term, especially in this information age. Neither do I like to settle for the returns of an index fund. I search for talented and/or lucky managers. I search for sectors that are on the rise. I keep them as long as they add value to my portfolio. When one stops adding value, then I replace it with another that does. It is no different than managing 'who-plays-when' in a hockey game.

It does not really matter which philosophy you follow. It does not matter whether an average active or and average passive investment does better. We have seen that even performing as well as the index does not ensure that your portfolio will survive as long as you might. So our goal should be to outperform the index.

So how are we going to build our winning "team" of mutual funds? How are we going to decide when a player is tired and needs "replacing"? How do we know the new "player" has a better chance of "scoring" than the one we are replacing?

Here is a method that I call "fingerprinting". Fingerprinting helps visualize fund behaviour separately in both rising and falling markets. It will assist you to evaluate fund excellence, regardless of whether you are a "buy-and-hold" investor or a "market-timer".

What is Fingerprinting?

Fingerprinting is a visual technique for analyzing mutual fund performance. It gives clear "buy", "hold" and "sell" signals.

An investment portfolio is a moving target, a work-in-progress. The fund manager must adjust its course as events occur. After each market crash, new patterns of strength and weakness develop. Fingerprinting allows you to detect these changes.

What is the Objective of Fingerprinting?

The Fingerprinting method has two objectives:

- To obtain the return of the index fund or the actively managed fund, whichever is higher,
- To catch sector trends.

A fund manager may excel in rising markets. Another may excel in falling markets. The Fingerprint chart depicts the performance of any portfolio manager, in two dimensions. In technical analysis jargon, this is called a "worm chart".

Figure 24: Fingerprint Chart Zones:

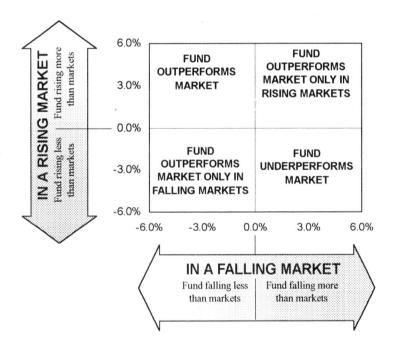

The chart is made up of four quadrants or zones. The significance of each zone is described in Figure 24.

In essence, the vertical scale of the Fingerprint Chart shows how a fund behaves relative to the rising market. The higher the point on the chart, the better is the fund at outperforming a rising market. The horizontal scale shows how the same fund behaves in a falling market. The further the point is to the left on the chart, the better the fund is at protecting itself in a falling market.

The benefits of Fingerprinting are:
- It is simple to maintain
- All data is readily available in the newspapers
- A single page graph describes the fund's performance visually in both rising and falling markets; you can observe several years of history on a single page.

How to Construct the Fingerprint Chart for your Mutual Fund:

The following example shows how to create a Fingerprint of your fund.

Step 1: Fill out the month and year in Column A, the growth of the benchmark index in Column B, and the growth of the fund in Column C.

Month/ Year	Index Monthly Growth	Fund Monthly Growth	Difference in		6-month Moving Average in	
			Up market	Down market	Up market	Down market
Col. A	Col. B	Col. C	Col. D	Col. E	Col. F	Col. G
Nov-95	4.7%	4.5%	-0.2	-		
Dec-95	1.4%	4.2%	2.8	-		
Jan-96	5.6%	6.0%	0.4	-		
Feb-96	-.5%	4.8%	-	-5.3		
Mar-96	1.0%	2.7%	1.7	-		
Apr-96	3.6%	3.6%	0.0	-	0.9	-5.3
May-96	2.1%	2.4%	0.3	-	1.0	-5.3
Jun-96	-3.6%	-0.5%	-	-3.1	0.6	-4.2
Jul-96	-2.2%	-1.2%	-	-1.0	0.7	-3.1
Aug-96	4.5%	7.9%	3.4	-	1.3	-2.1
Sep-96	3.1%	8.8%	5.7	-	2.3	-2.1
Oct-96	5.9%	6.3%	0.4	-	2.4	-2.1

Step 2:   If Column B is a positive number (i.e. market is up), take the difference of the fund growth and index growth (Column C minus Column B) and write it in Column D. If Column B is a negative number (i.e. market is down), write the difference (Column B minus Column C) in Column E.

You need at least six months of data to start your fingerprint chart. Repeat Step 2 until the first six lines are completed.

Step 3:   Calculate the average of the last six numbers in Column D and write it in Column F. When calculating the average, if there is a "-" in the box (i.e. no number in the box) do not include it in the calculation. For instance, the average in April 1996 in Column F is calculated as (-0.2 + 2.8 + 0.4 + 1.7 + 0.0) / 5 = 0.94. We did not include February 1996 because that month was blank in Column D. Since we had only five numbers to average, we divided the total by 5 and not by 6.

Step 4:   Calculate the average of the last six numbers in Column E and write them in Column G. Use only non-blank numbers. For example, the average in April 1996 in Column F is calculated as (-5.3) / 1 = -5.3. We included only February 1996 because that was the only[23] non-blank number in Column E.

Step 5:   Plot the values of Columns F and G on the graph[24]. The value in Column F measures the relative performance of the fund in a rising market. It is plotted on the vertical scale. The value in Column G measures the relative performance of the fund in a falling market, so it is plotted on the horizontal scale. Join each new point with the previous month's point.

---

[23]   If this column is blank for all previous six months, then there is no average number to calculate. If that is the case, just carry forward the previous average number to current month.

[24]   Hint: For diversified funds, use a graph range between -6% to +6%. For sector, country and similar volatile funds, use a graph range between –25% to +25%.

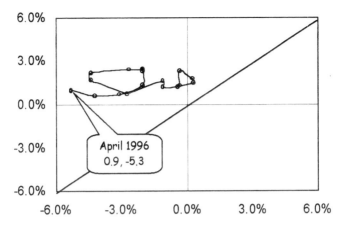

Figure 25: Fingerprint of the example fund:

The location of the Fingerprint reveals whether the fund is outperforming the markets. In this case, Figure 25 illustrates the Fingerprint of the fund is in the upper-left quadrant, meaning it has been outperforming its benchmark both in up and down markets.

We observe that this fund has been outperforming its benchmark index between 0.6% and 3% per month in rising markets (vertical scale). We can also observe that it has been outperforming its benchmark by 0% to 5% per month in falling markets (horizontal scale). This is a remarkable performance. I would hold this fund in my portfolio as long as its fingerprint remains there.

Figure 26 shows examples of idealized price charts of the fund and its benchmark, and each corresponding fingerprint chart.

106

Figure 26: Examples of idealized price charts and their corresponding fingerprint.

Price Chart: ⟹ **Fingerprint Chart:**

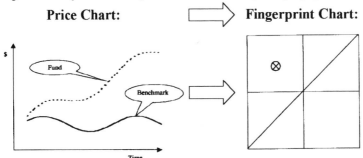

Fund outperforms the index in rising and falling markets
(typically, a well managed active fund)

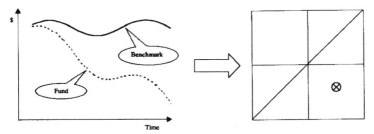

Fund underperforms the index in rising and falling markets
(typically, a mismanaged active fund)

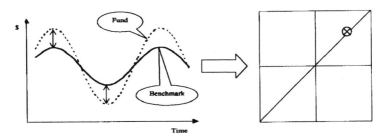

Fund outperforms the index in rising markets and underperforms the index in falling markets
(typically, an actively managed agressive fund)

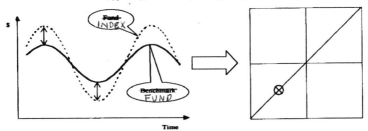

Fund outperforms the index in falling markets and underperforms the index in rising markets
(typically, an actively managed defensive or a balanced fund)

The shape of the Fingerprint Chart can reveal a fund's style. Let's look at different fund styles.

Index Funds:

Index funds replicate the underlying index. They may be holding the index or they may hold the stocks that are in the index. The fund neither outperforms, nor under-performs the index. Therefore, we expect the Fingerprint of an index fund to be a single dot right at the centre of our chart.

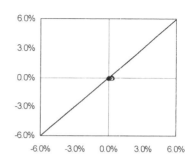

Figure 27: Fingerprint Chart of an Index Fund

Figure 27 depicts the Fingerprint of a typical index fund. The Fingerprint is ever so slightly in the "underperform" zone because of the effect of management expenses.

Closet Index Funds:

The managers of these funds, under the guise of actively managing their fund, actually mimic the index while collecting generous management fees. This strategy protects the manager as well. When the fund follows the markets down, blame the markets. When the fund goes up with the markets, the manager looks good. The Fingerprint of a closet-index fund is not too dissimilar to the Fingerprint of an index fund.

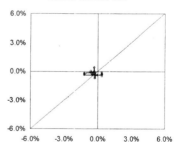

Figure 28: Fingerprint Chart of a Closet- Index Fund

Figure 28 depicts a typical "closet-index" fund.

Sector Rotators:

This style is also called "top-down". A "top-down" manager overweighs the fund's stock holdings in sectors which he thinks will outperform the market. The rest of the fund's holdings are usually similar to the underlying index.

108

One can expect the fingerprint of a "top-down" fund to be a hybrid of the Fingerprint of an index fund and the Fingerprint of the overweighed sector.

Figure 29 depicts the Fingerprint of a typical sector rotator fund. The Fingerprint indicates this fund outperformed the benchmark during most of the time. The Fingerprint covers a larger area indicating swings in the overweighting of different sectors at different times.

Aggressive Funds:

Aggressive funds tend to do better in rising markets. Their Fingerprint may appear in a band that runs vertically on the Fingerprint chart.

Figure 30 depicts an aggressive fund.

Defensive Funds:

Defensive funds tend to do better in falling markets. Their Fingerprint may appear in a "band" that runs horizontal on the Fingerprint chart.

Figure 31 depicts a defensive fund.

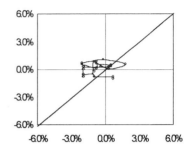

Figure 29: Fingerprint Chart of a Sector Rotator Fund

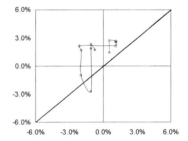

Figure 30: Fingerprint Chart of an Aggressively Managed Fund

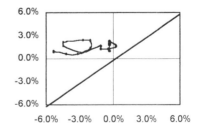

Figure 31: Fingerprint Chart of a Defensively Managed Fund

Buy, Hold or Sell:

Now that we have covered the shape of the Fingerprint as it relates to the fund style, let's see how we can use Fingerprinting to help us to make better investment choices.

In essence, you want to own a fund if its Fingerprint is in the top-left zone of the chart. Some well-managed funds leave Fingerprints in this area for several years. However, eventually most funds either become too big and inefficient or their managers leave for greener pastures.

An action signal (buy, hold or sell) is generated depending in which zone the most recent point of the Fingerprint is located. If the point is located in the top left zone, it is in the "buy zone". As long as it stays above the diagonal line, it is a "hold". If the point moves below the diagonal line, it is in the "sell zone".

Market Risk:

The Fingerprinting method covers the fund risk, which is the fund's underperforming the index. There is another risk and that is the market risk.

Markets occasionally crash. More often, they experience corrections. Investors accept this as a fact of life. In bull markets, crashes and corrections are opportunities to buy. In bear markets, it is the opposite; rallies are opportunities to sell.

No one can predict the severity of a market crash. It may be 90% as happened during 1929 and the early 1930's. Since the spring of 2000, the NASDAQ index has lost about 70% from its peak. During August 1998, the Toronto Stock Exchange Index, TSE300, plummeted 30%. Japanese markets crashed in 1990, and twelve years later, they were still 70% below their peak. These events have as much to do with the collective investor psychology as any of the other reasons: economics, demographics, cycles, or the full moon.

There are five possible outcomes of any investment:
- Large loss
- Small loss
- Breakeven
- Small gain
- Large gain

Obviously, eliminating the large losses will give you better portfolio returns. For each fund I calculate a price that is below the current price. If the fund price drops below that level then I sell the fund. This price level is called a "trailing stop". For diversified equity funds and balanced funds, I take the highest recent price and set my trailing stop 8% below it. For sector funds and volatile funds, I leave more room for the fund price to fluctuate by using 10%. When the unit value of a fund goes below its trailing stop, I then switch the fund to the money market to protect it from larger losses.

Following this simple technical procedure as outlined above may give you a better return on the equity side of your portfolio.

When you are in a bull market, Fingerprinting your funds may appear to be as useless as using radar on a clear day, but that is exactly what prudent captains do. They practice in ideal conditions. When the visibility becomes zero, as always happens when markets are changing their trend, you need to have practised.

The Fingerprinting technique may cost you two or three hours of homework each month but it may reward you with several additional years of retirement income.

Chapter 10

Wrapping-Up

Almost all of us in the financial business, including advisors, brokers, financial planners etc., use the standard retirement plan model as the basis of estimating our clients' needs during retirement. Since they are used so commonly and indisputably, when I started my research I was hoping I would find some way of confirming their merit.

The opposite occured. I observed in case after case that the existing retirement plan model was consistently far too optimistic.

> *Tip #1: Avoid using the standard financial plan model projections for your retirement portfolio. They do not reflect the historic reality within an acceptable margin of error.*
>
> *If you must use the standard retirement plan, then you can obtain a more realistic result by entering a higher income into the standard financial plan model. This reduces the projected portfolio life to a level that commensurates with historic experience.*
>
> *Whatever your income requirement is at the time of your retirement, increase it by a third and enter this as your income required. For example if your income need from your portfolio is $45,000, then enter $60,000 into the model. ($45,000 x 1.333 = $60,000). Doing so will decrease the projected portfolio life sufficiently, rendering it more in line with historic performance.*

My next step was looking at the Monte Carlo model. For reasons mentioned earlier, it also did not fit my criteria of a reliable and sound method of estimation.

> *Tip #2: If you want to include random fluctuations, your model should take into account the effects of market cycles. You may want to visit my site (www.cotar.org) and download my retirement simulator. It does not address the extended bull/bear markets but it does chart the minimum portfolio life based on the empirical data of the last century. Use it at your own risk.*

Having found no comfort in using the standard retirement plan and the Monte Carlo model, my only remaining choice was to develop a model based on empirical data. As addressed in various tables throughout this book, they demonstrate what we can expect from the markets based on historic data.

Figures 32 and 33 show the minimum and average portfolio life respectively, based on optimum portfolios as shown in Table 5 of Chapter 6.

Figure 32. Minimum Portfolio Life (years) for retirement years between 1900-1999, based on optimum portfolios as shown in Table 5.

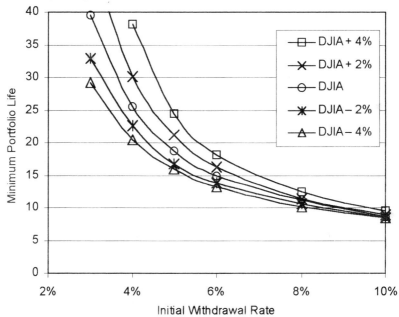

Figure 33. Average Portfolio Life (years) for retirement years between 1900-1999, based on optimum portfolios as shown on Table 5.

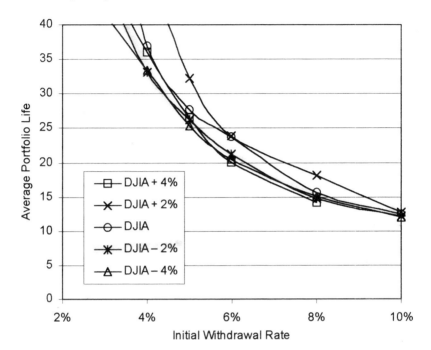

Tip #3: If you want your income portfolio to last at least 30 years, do not withdraw more than 3.5% initially (withdrawals are adjusted annually for inflation after the first year). If the equity portion of your portfolio has been outperforming the index then you can increase the initial withdrawal rate to 4%.

That means, at the beginning of your retirement you should have accumulated capital that is about 30 times that of your first year's withdrawal.

Keep in mind; this is only based on the available historic data of 1900-1999. The performance of capital markets may well be different in the future.

What are the most potent boosters of portfolio longevity?

1. The Withdrawal Rate:

The lower the withdrawal rate; the longer the portfolio life. Increasing the withdrawal rate from 4% to 6% can reduce the portfolio life by up to 80%.

> *Tip #4:* *If your withdrawal rate indicates depletion of your portfolio sooner than your life expectancy, you should seriously consider buying a life annuity. If you are worried about the loss of your estate value, you can buy annuities with a minimum payment term, such as 10 years.*
>
> *On the other hand, if at anytime your current withdrawal rate falls below 2% (perhaps the stock market had a good year) you may consider taking some of your capital from your portfolio and using that money to buy a life annuity. This will reduce your income need from your portfolio by the amount of the annuity income. This may extend your portfolio life and also increase the estate value of your portfolio in the long term. During a mega bull market, this strategy may allow you to buy sufficient annuity contracts so that you don't need an income from your portfolio any longer. One of the surest ways of preserving a portfolio is to convert it from an "income" portfolio into an "investment" portfolio[25].*
>
> *Each individual case is different and should be analysed thoroughly. There is no cookie-cutter solution for this.*

---

[25] A portfolio is defined as an income portfolio if you take out a regular income. If you don't take out regular income then it is an investment portfolio.

2. Strategic Asset Allocation:

Even if you use a simple asset mix of 60% fixed income with 40% equity and rebalance it every four years at the end of the U. S. Presidential election year, you can just about double the minimum portfolio life compared to an all-equity portfolio.

3. Outperforming the index:

This has a large contribution to the life of your portfolio, especially at lower withdrawal rates. If you have time and can succesfully outperform the index, then you can increase the longevity of your portfolio by between 20% and 100%.

4. Optimizing Asset Mix and Rebalancing:

Optimizing the asset mix and rebalancing for your individual income needs can add up to 10% to an average portfolio life. In most cases that means rebalancing once every four years instead of annually.

5. Investing in Equities Gradually Over Time:

Instead of implementing the asset allocation all at once, if you dollar-cost-average the equities over four years based on the U.S. Presidential election cycle, you can add up to 15% to your minimum portfolio life.

I hope you are now better equipped to design your retirement strategy than when you started reading this book.

Happy Retirement!

Appendix A

Data

Column A: End of year

Column B: Interest rate, courtesy of "Market Volatility" by Robert J. Shiller, MIT Press [1997], page pp 440-441, Data Series 4

Column C: Annual Change of DJIA, %

Column D: Annual Inflation, % (U.S. Bureau of Labor Statistics wholesale price index for the years between 1900 -1913, the consumer price index after 1913)

A	B	C	D	A	B	C	D	A	B	C	D
1899	3.4	9.2	7.4	1933	1.5	66.7	0.8	1967	5.6	15.2	3.0
1900	4.6	7.0	8.1	1934	1.0	4.1	1.5	1968	6.2	4.3	4.7
1901	4.3	-8.7	-2.6	1935	0.8	38.5	3.0	1969	8.1	-15.2	6.2
1902	4.7	-0.4	6.2	1936	0.8	24.8	1.4	1970	9.1	4.8	5.6
1903	5.5	-23.6	2.5	1937	0.9	-32.8	2.9	1971	5.7	6.1	3.3
1904	4.3	41.7	2.5	1938	0.9	28.1	-2.8	1972	4.6	14.6	3.4
1905	4.2	38.2	-2.4	1939	0.6	-2.9	0.0	1973	7.9	-16.6	8.7
1906	5.5	-1.9	3.5	1940	0.6	-12.7	0.7	1974	11.0	-27.6	12.3
1907	6.2	-37.7	5.5	1941	0.5	-15.4	9.9	1975	7.2	38.3	6.9
1908	5.3	46.6	-4.2	1942	0.6	7.6	9.0	1976	5.7	17.9	4.9
1909	3.7	15.0	7.8	1943	0.7	13.8	3.0	1977	5.3	-17.3	6.7
1910	5.3	-17.9	4.1	1944	0.7	12.1	2.3	1978	7.8	-3.2	9.0
1911	4.0	0.4	-7.8	1945	0.8	26.7	2.2	1979	10.9	4.2	13.3
1912	4.4	7.6	6.5	1946	0.8	-8.1	18.1	1980	11.4	14.9	12.5
1913	5.7	-10.3	0.9	1947	1.0	2.2	8.8	1981	17.6	-9.2	8.9
1914	4.6	-30.7	1.0	1948	1.4	-2.1	3.0	1982	14.6	19.6	3.8
1915	3.7	81.7	2.0	1949	1.6	12.9	-2.1	1983	9.4	20.3	3.8
1916	3.6	-4.2	12.6	1950	1.3	17.6	5.9	1984	11.1	-3.7	3.9
1917	4.3	-21.7	18.1	1951	2.1	14.4	6.0	1985	8.4	27.7	3.8
1918	6.0	10.5	20.4	1952	2.4	8.4	0.8	1986	7.3	22.6	1.1
1919	5.4	30.5	14.5	1953	2.6	-3.8	0.7	1987	6.6	2.3	4.4
1920	7.3	-32.9	2.6	1954	1.8	44.0	-0.7	1988	7.9	11.9	4.4
1921	7.4	12.7	-10.8	1955	1.8	20.8	0.4	1989	9.1	27.0	4.6
1922	4.6	21.7	-2.3	1956	3.2	2.3	3.0	1990	8.2	-4.3	6.1
1923	5.0	-3.3	2.4	1957	3.9	-12.8	2.9	1991	5.9	20.3	3.1
1924	4.3	26.2	0.0	1958	2.5	34.0	1.8	1992	3.8	4.2	2.9
1925	3.9	30.0	3.5	1959	3.7	16.4	1.7	1993	3.3	13.7	2.7
1926	4.3	0.3	-1.1	1960	4.3	-9.3	1.4	1994	5.0	2.1	2.7
1927	4.3	28.8	-2.3	1961	2.9	18.7	0.7	1995	6.0	33.5	2.5
1928	4.6	48.2	-1.2	1962	3.4	-10.8	1.3	1996	5.5	26.0	3.3
1929	6.0	-17.2	0.6	1963	3.5	17.0	1.6	1997	5.7	22.6	1.7
1930	4.2	-33.8	-6.4	1964	4.1	14.6	1.0	1998	5.4	16.1	1.6
1931	2.4	-52.7	-9.3	1965	4.5	10.9	1.9	1999	5.5	25.2	2.7
1932	3.4	-23.1	-10.3	1966	5.4	-18.9	3.5				

27-89
5.7

Appendix B

Retirement Cash Flow Worksheet

Here is a worksheet to help you to estimate your income needs after retirement. Follow these steps:

1. Estimate all of your annual expenses after your retirement.
2. Estimate your annual income from all sources, excepting your retirement savings portfolio.
3. Calculate the shortfall, if any, that needs to be provided by your retirement savings portfolio.
4. Calculate how much you need in your retirement savings portfolio at the time of retirement, to finance any shortfall.

1. Estimate your annual retirement expenses at the start of your retirement (use today's dollars):

Housing	Monthly Expense $	Annual Expense $
Mortgage[26]	_____	_____
(Last payment date of the mortgage _____)		
Rent	_____	_____
Condominium Fees	_____	_____
Property Insurance	_____	_____
Heat	_____	_____
Water	_____	_____
Electricity	_____	_____
Security & Alarm Service	_____	_____
Maintenance & Repairs	_____	_____
Other	_____	_____
Other	_____	_____
TOTAL Housing Expenses		_____

---

[26]   Do not include mortgage expenses if the mortgage is to be paid off before your retirement.

	Monthly Monthly Expense $	Annual Annual Expense $
Household and Living Expenses:		
Food, Groceries	_____	_____
Dry Cleaning & Laundry	_____	_____
Decorating & Painting	_____	_____
Carpet Cleaning	_____	_____
Gardening	_____	_____
Pool	_____	_____
Pet Care	_____	_____
Kennel	_____	_____
Maid Service	_____	_____
Computer Equipment & Maintenance	_____	_____
Pocket Money	_____	_____
Clothing	_____	_____
Footwear	_____	_____
Dependent Support 1	_____	_____
Dependent Support 2	_____	_____
Anniversary Gifts	_____	_____
Seasonal Gifts	_____	_____
Other Gifts	_____	_____
Donations	_____	_____
Other	_____	_____
Other	_____	_____
TOTAL Household And Living Expenses		_____

	Monthly Expense $	Annual Expense $

Transportation Expenses:

Car Loan Payments .... _____ _____

(Last payment date of the car loan _____)

Lease Payments .... _____ _____

Maintenance & Repairs .... _____ _____

License Fees .... _____ _____

Gasoline .... _____ _____

Oil Change .... _____ _____

Parking .... _____ _____

Car Insurance .... _____ _____

Car Rental .... _____ _____

Public Transportation .... _____ _____

Other .... _____ _____

TOTAL Transportation Expenses .... _____

Investment Expenses:

Investment Loan Payments .... _____ _____

(Last payment date of the investment loan _____)

Accounting Fees .... _____ _____

Legal Fees .... _____ _____

Other Professional Fees .... _____ _____

Investment Related Subscriptions .... _____ _____

Other .... _____ _____

Other .... _____ _____

Parking .... _____ _____

TOTAL Transportation Expenses .... _____

Health Care Expenses:	Monthly Expense $	Annual Expense $
Hair Care	_____	_____
Beauty Supplies	_____	_____
Personal Care	_____	_____
Manicure, Pedicure	_____	_____
Doctors	_____	_____
Dentists	_____	_____
Prescription Drugs	_____	_____
Vitamins & Nutritional Supplements	_____	_____
Visiting Home Care / Home Aid	_____	_____
Live-in Home Care	_____	_____
Nursing Care	_____	_____
Medical & Support Equipment	_____	_____
Other	_____	_____
Other	_____	_____
TOTAL Health Care Expenses		_____

Communication Expenses:	Monthly Expense $	Annual Expense $
Telephone	_____	_____
Mobile Phone	_____	_____
Cable TV	_____	_____
Satellite TV	_____	_____
Pay TV	_____	_____
Internet Access	_____	_____
Other	_____	_____
Other	_____	_____
TOTAL Communication Expenses		_____

	Monthly Expense $	Annual Expense $
Personal Insurance Expenses:		
Term Life Insurance 1	_____	_____
Term Life Insurance 2	_____	_____
Permanent Life Insurance 1	_____	_____
Permanent Life Insurance 2	_____	_____
Disability Insurance 1	_____	_____
Disability Insurance 2	_____	_____
Long Term Care Insurance 1	_____	_____
Long Term Care Insurance 2	_____	_____
Critical Illness Insurance 1	_____	_____
Critical Illness Insurance 2	_____	_____
Private Health / Dental Care 1	_____	_____
Private Health / Dental Care 1	_____	_____
Other	_____	_____
Other	_____	_____
TOTAL Personal Insurance Expenses		_____

	Monthly Expense $	Annual Expense $

Recreational & Entertainment Expenses:

	Monthly Expense $	Annual Expense $
Clubs	_____	_____
Travel	_____	_____
Campimg	_____	_____
Sports Equipment	_____	_____
Books...	_____	_____
Newspapers, Magazines	_____	_____
Adult Education	_____	_____
Hobbies 1	_____	_____
Hobbies 2	_____	_____
Hobbies 3	_____	_____
Dining Out	_____	_____
Catering	_____	_____
Entertaining at home	_____	_____
Theatre, Ballet, Concerts	_____	_____
Sports Events	_____	_____
Tobacco	_____	_____
Other	_____	_____
Other	_____	_____
TOTAL Recreational & Entertainment Expenses		_____

Annual
Expense $

Add up all of your Expenses:

Housing .... _____

Household and Living Expenses .... _____

Transportation Expenses .... _____

Investment Expenses .... _____

Health Care Expenses .... _____

Communication Expenses...................................... _____

Personal Insurance Expenses .... _____

Recreational & Entertainment Expenses .... _____

TOTAL Expenses before Taxes .... _____

Estimated Taxes .... _____

TOTAL EXPENSES IN TODAY'S DOLLARS ...... _____

Calculate Total Expenses in Future Dollars:

Multiply the Total Expenses in today's dollars (from previous page) with the Inflation Multiplier from the table below.

Inflation Multiplier Table:

Years from Retirement	Inflation 2%	Inflation 3%	Inflation 4%	Inflation 5%
0	1.00	1.00	1.00	1.00
2	1.04	1.06	1.08	1.10
4	1.08	1.13	1.17	1.22
6	1.13	1.19	1.27	1.34
8	1.17	1.27	1.37	1.48
10	1.22	1.34	1.48	1.63
15	1.35	1.56	1.80	2.08

Total Expenses in future Dollars = $_____ ✗ _____

Total Expenses in future Dollars = $ _____
(at the time of retirement)

Other Potential Expense Considerations:

- Buy a car every _____ years starting with the first year of retirement until age _____.

- Get rid of the family car at age _____, reducing transportation expenses, increasing taxi/bus fare expenses.

- Increase Health Care Expenses by $ _____ after age _____.

- Increase Health Care Expenses again by $ _____ after age _____.

- Decrease Travel expenses by $ _____ after age _____.

2. Estimate your annual income from all sources at the time of your retirement (future dollars), excluding income from your retirement savings portfolio :

Annual

Employment Related:
Income $

Employment of Spouse .... _____

  (From: _____ Until : _____)

Part Time Employment .... _____

  (From: _____ Until : _____)

Part Time Employment .... _____

  (From: _____ Until : _____)

Company Pension 1 .... _____

  (From: _____ Until : _____)

Company Pension 2 .... _____

  (From: _____ Until : _____)

Company Pension 3 .... _____

  (From: _____ Until : _____)

Company Pension 4 .... _____

  (From: _____ Until : _____)

Other .... _____

  (From: _____ Until : _____)

Other .... _____

  (From: _____ Until : _____)

TOTAL Employment-Related Retirement Income .... _____

	Annual Income $
Government Pensions and Benefits:	
Pension Self	_____
Pension Spouse	_____
Old Age / Senior Benefits Self	_____
Old Age / Senior Benefits Spouse	_____
Other Government Benefits Self	_____
Other Government Benefits Spouse	_____
TOTAL Government Benefits	_____
Other Income:	
Rental Income	_____
Royalty Income	_____
Annuity	_____
Annuity	_____
Other	_____
Other	_____
TOTAL Other Income	_____

Annual
Income $

Add up all of your Retirement Income:

Employment-Related ....   _____

Government Benefits ....   _____

Other ....   _____

TOTAL Projected Income at Retirement ....   _____

3. Calculate the income shortfall that needs to be provided by your retirement savings portfolio :

<A> Total Projected Income at Retirement ....   _____

<B> Total Expenses in Future Dollars ....   _____

• If amount <A> is larger than amount <B>, then you have surplus, you don't need to draw income from your portfolio.

• If amount <A> is less then amount <B>, then calculate shortfall

  Shortfall equals Amount <B> less amount <A> ....   _____

  (The shortfall is the amount that you need
  to withdraw from your retirement savings
  annually)

4. Calculate how much you need in your retirement savings portfolio at the time of retirement:

Multiply the shortfall from the previous page with the "Multiplier" given for your/your spouse's life expectancy to estimate how much you need to have in your retirement portfolio at the time of your retirement.

Life Expectancy after Retirement (years)	Multiplier
10	12
20	22
30	30
40	35

Portfolio Value Required = shortfall ✘ multiplier

Portfolio Value Required = $_____ ✘ _____

Portfolio Value Required = $ _____
(at the time of retirement)

Appendix C
Retirement Spreadsheet:

An easy way of estimating the longevity of your portfolio is by downloading my retirement simulator spreadsheet from my site: www.cotar.org

> (Warning: The retirement spreadsheet is based on historic data. Future values will be different. Use at your own risk. Always consult with your advisor.)

You can enter your changing income needs on a yearly basis. You can also add lump sum expenses such as buying a car every so often or an expected inheritance at some time during your retirement.

Retirement Case Example:

Bob is 63 years old and retiring now. Jane is 56 years old. She is married to Bob. Jane is planning to work 6 more years. They have saved a total of $355,000 in their retirement portfolios.

They calculated all their expenses and income needs. They came to the following conclusions:

- Bob needs $8,000/year from their savings while Jane is still working, until she is 62.

- After accounting for their pension income, they still need $35,000/year from their savings after Jane retires and until the mortgage is paid off at the end of second year after Jane's retirement. In other words, they need to increase their withdrawals by $27,000 after Jane is 62.

- Their mortgage will be paid off when Jane is 64. After that they will reduce their withdrawals by $12,000/year.

- They need to replace Jane's car when she is 67 years old. They now use one car only and they figure a car will cost them $40,000 then. They expect to replace this car six years later, which will cost them another $55,000. This car should keep them going until they cannot drive anymore.

- When Bob is 72 years old, he expects an inheritance from his youngest uncle. He estimates that his share of the estate might be $120,000 at that time.

Calculate how long their portfolio will last, based on the worst-case scenario during the twentieth century.

First download the spreadsheet. For your convinience, its cells (boxes) are color coded: You can enter information only in the green boxes. If you try to change any other box, you'll get an error message.

The spreadsheet is made up of two parts.

The top part allows you to enter the general information: Here you can input the value of your portfolio at the time of your retirement, and how much income you need to withdraw in your first year of retirement. You can also change the inflation rate, and you can choose whether or not you want random volatility in your calculation.

For our example, we enter the value of Bob's portfolio at the time of his retirement as $355,000.

Bob retires first and he needs only $8,000/year from his portfolio until Jane retiresafter six years. Therefore, we enter $8,000 as the income requirement from the portfolio in the first year.

The program automatically adjusts this for inflation, which we left at a default value of 3.5%.

Here is how the input for the top part looks:

BOB AND JANE'S STARTING PORTFOLIO:

What is the value of your portfolio at the start of your retirement?	$355,000
How much money do you want to withdraw from your investments during the first year?	$8,000
How much of an annual inflation rate do you want to apply to your withdrawals?	3.5%

The lower part of the spreadsheet allows you to enter the cash flow events year by year.

• We adjust the increased expenses by $27,000 as Jane is retiring in six years. This increases the withdrawals from the portfolio for each year afterwards.

• We adjust the decreased expenses by $12,000, since the mortgage will be paid off when Jane is 64 years of age. This decreases the withdrawals from the portfolio for each year afterwards.

• We enter lump sum deposits, such as Bob's expected inheritance.

• As well, we enter lump sum withdrawals, such as buying a car.

The table below shows how this information is entered into the spreadsheet:

BOB AND JANE'S VARYING CASH FLOW:

Age Bob	Age Jane	Lump Sum Deposit $	Lump Sum With-drawal $	Increased Expense $	Reduced Expense $	Notes:
63	56					BOB RETIRES
64	57					
65	58					
66	59					
67	60					
68	61					
69	62			$27,000		JANE RETIRES
70	63					
71	64				$12,000	MORTGAGE PAID-OFF
72	65	$120,000				BOB'S INHERITANCE
73	66					
74	67		$40,000			BUY A CAR
75	68					
76	69					
77	70					
78	71					
79	72					
80	73		$55,000			BUY A CAR
81	74					

Next, observe the chart:

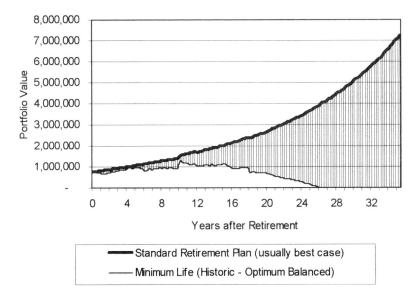

Years after Retirement

━━━ Standard Retirement Plan (usually best case)
──── Minimum Life (Historic - Optimum Balanced)

Looking at the chart, you can see that in the worst case this portfolio lasted between 25 and 28 years[27]. We disregard the upper line, the standard retirement plan, because it usually shows the best-case situation. We want to design our portfolio based on a worst-case situation.

Say Bob and Jane want their portfolio to last 30 years. How much should they have saved at the beginning of Bob's retirement? To answer this, we increase the portfolio value at the start of the retirement (using the top part of the spreadsheet) until the minimum life shows 30 years. Doing so, we find that the answer is: $300,000.

After Bob's retirement, only Jane is working. How much should she save until her retirement, so that their portfolio lasts for 30 years? To answer that, we fill in the lump sum deposit column for the first 6 years. We change the amounts until the minimum portfolio life shows 30 years. As it works out, if Jane saved $6,000 each year until her retirement, they can then achieve this objective.

---

[27] If you keep your finger on "recalculate" button (F9), you will notice the random motion.

Notes:

Notes:

Index